SELLING
MADE
SIMPLE

Steve Sullivan

HRD Press, Inc., Amherst, Massachusetts

Published by: HRD Press, Inc.
22 Amherst Road
Amherst, MA 01002
800-822-2801 (U.S. and Canada)
413-253-3488
413-253-3490 (fax)
http://www.hrdpress.com

ISBN 0-87425-586-4

Editorial services by Joan Hiam
Production services by CompuDesign
Cover design by Donna Thibault-Wong

When you walk the path of least resistance you abandon
the opportunity to find out who you are.

Steve Sullivan

To Linus Cooke,
no one sells better.

CONTENTS

PROLOGUE

This book is about selling, pure and simple. It started out as a 600 page dissertation on the subject, but when I realized it wouldn't be sold by the pound, I edited out everything that was meaningless and the pages you have remaining say as much about selling as needs to be said.

The thoughts presented are my own. I'm not sure any of them are original. I've read the books, I know the buzz words, and I'm aware that there are countless ways to open and close a sale. Sales expertise is everywhere and that's why I'm confused.

Given the abundance of material that is available, it's perplexing that so many people don't sell. The actions that need to be taken are never seen. Part of it can be blamed on marketing, a basic tenet of which involves one's ability to differentiate oneself.

If you want to sell a book, a sales manual, or a sales training program, your information needs to look different from what's already in print. Vocabulary becomes important. How many different ways can we label a buyer, sales environment, or method of asking for some business?

These thoughts, presented under the heading of Motivational Acceleration, are my attempt to simplify a process many have made overly complex. The presentation is conceptual in nature. My concern is that you understand the issues at play. I don't care what idiosyncratic approach you take to building successful relationships. Motivational Acceleration embraces a salesman's desire to think and act situationally.

The operative word is action. When you act you learn, when you learn you adjust, when you adjust you fine-tune methodology. You'll discover as you refine your approach that the results will come with dramatic swiftness.

Now before we go any further, let's come to an understanding. When I use the word salesman, I'm doing so in a gender-free capacity: Salesman as in mankind. There are salesmen and saleswomen. Salesmen act upon buyers. The buyer has the ability to give something to the seller. It could be time, money, effort, or consideration. The buyer is your target of opportunity.

The salesman on the other hand, is an offensive agent. He or she initiates the action and is desirous of having the buyer make a move that is in his or her best interest. For a perfect sales situation to exist, both parties' interests need to be equally served. But this isn't a perfect world and this book isn't about fairness. It's about motivating another individual to give you what you want, in your professional life and in your personal life.

It seems reasonable to me that the more accelerated the pace at which you achieve your goals, the more you will accomplish. Motivational Acceleration is about a lot of things, none of which are more important than compressing the time it takes to make things happen.

AN OBSERVATION

It's only a matter of time before youthful idealism passes, and you start to realize that success in life is not a given. If you are going to make an impact, there is a window of opportunity in which to do it. Whatever you are going to achieve will have to happen within defined time boundaries. At some point your productive years will come to an end.

Given that fact, it's been interesting to observe at what stage in a person's existence, if at all, he gets turned on, takes charge, and tries to accomplish something. With many people, it doesn't happen until they are a long way into life's journey. Alexander the Great must have known he would die at 32. If he wanted to conquer the world he needed to do it quickly. History is populated by individuals whose ignition spark came at an early age. We all enjoy the benefits of their effort and accomplishment.

Others never live up to their potential. Their lives are characterized by one failure after another and they don't understand why. On the surface they appear to have as much going for them as anyone else, but nothing of any consequence ever happens. Success in most things escapes them. Little did they know that the slightest behavioral modification would have made all the difference.

If you chronicled their lives, you would find the foundation for failure was built early on. In adolescence, things came easily. Mom and Dad provided. The more that was provided in the formative years, the greater the optimism that things would always be that way. From youth, many carry with them a belief that things will proceed upward because they exist. A convoluted manifest destiny or divine intervention will govern what happens. Their future success is secure, and nothing much is required. A cornucopia of rewarding experiences is waiting to be harvested, just take your pick.

As time marches inexorably forward, the muted visions of a childhood fantasy take on a sharper edge. The image crystallizes. There is no Porsche in the driveway. The house on the hill resembles a two-bedroom apartment and you haven't had a promotion in years. Is it time for a wake-up call?

I suspect you wouldn't have purchased this book if you weren't looking for self-improvement. But I'd also bet that you harbor a view that there is plenty of time to get started, that the important sales of your life are at some distant juncture. I suggest that the quicker you get going the better you will do. I say this because the greatest opportunity you may encounter might present itself tomorrow. Not knowing how to capitalize on it could prove costly.

When I was younger, I viewed my future and how it would progress in stages. I thought that there would be a clear delineation between when one part ended and the next began. I saw my life's journey as Robert Frost might have seen it in his famous poem, *The Road Not Taken*. That road meanders along until it finally splits and when it does you have a decision to make. Do you take the left fork or go right? I envisioned that as I walked the road I would see the juncture in the distance. There would be plenty of time to prepare.

In reflecting back on my life I now see that most of the opportunities and successes I've had seemed to sprout from something unexpected. They materialized quickly and if anything were to be made of them, time was of the essence. If I couldn't get the fish to bite, I couldn't bring it in.

The fact is the road splits hundreds of times in one's life. There will be myriad encounters with each one having the potential to provide something that moves you in a different, more rewarding and exciting direction. Acceptance, inclusion, reward, and recognition rests in the minds of others. How you influence their willingness to support your efforts is up to you. You are in control of your actions, but recognize, it is the actions of others that will determine where you end up. Until you understand the impact of behavior, you will never achieve as much as you could.

INTRODUCTION

Embrace the opportunity to fail; failure has always been a better teacher than success.

Do you spend a lot of time thinking about success? I do. Most people do. I'm constantly evaluating my situation in relationship to where I thought I would be, where I want to be. I'll bet you do the same thing, and in doing so, you can't help but compare yourself to others. It is a relative world we live in. There will always be individuals who accomplish less and people who accomplish more. What should be noted is, often, there is very little correlation among hard work, intelligence, ability, and success.

Everywhere you look there are people who have achieved greater financial gain, job satisfaction, and emotional nourishment than yourself. Seemingly, they are more successful, and success in my mind is a life characterized by a higher level of participation, accomplishment, and reinforcement.

What determines success from failure? In an earlier era we assumed the movers and shakers were tapped for greatness because they were superior. A hundred years ago, the communication age was a Jules Verne fantasy. Information moved slowly, if at all. You could blunder and no one knew.

Today, the message moves at the speed of light. Change is accelerating at unprecedented levels. Technology has brought the circus to our living room, bathroom, and all rooms in between. Data supports the paradigm. "Buzz" exploits the concept. Operate at anything less than a "nanosecond" and you're bye-bye buster.

A brief look at evolutionary processes punctuates the point. The Food and Gathering Stage of human existence occupied millions of years. The Agrarian Period was compressed to millenniums. The Industrial Age came and went in little more than a century. The Era of Technology was reduced to decades and, holy cow, in the Information Age the entire world could change tomorrow. There are those that would tell you, if you're not online, you're inline, for disaster.

Hold on a second. While I would agree that technological innovation has taken a quantum leap forward, people haven't. I'm not sure the emotional make-up of Joe and Jane Doe has changed at all. I've found that the behaviors that impressed individuals a hundred years ago impress them today and will impress them a hundred years from now. Not everything hinges on the introduction of a new microchip. When dealing with "homo erectus" you may want to eschew a broadband strategy in favor of civility.

It is possible that selling in the future will mirror the past: That salesmen who will enjoy the greatest success will embrace humanistic coins of the realm. And that we shouldn't substitute complex techniques, gimmicks, and academic theories for behaviors that exhibit respect, trust, loyalty, support, care, and kindness.

Let's briefly get back to those individuals who we know are no better than us, but for some reason have accomplished more. If we examined ten cases of success and juxtaposed one against another, we would see variability in how that success came about. There would be differences in physical appearance, knowledge, focus, sense of urgency, and commitment. Is there a common denominator? Absolutely, their ability to sell.

Are you wondering whether you are a salesman? Some people are frightened by the term. They may not have figured out yet that everyone lives by selling something. You may not have "salesman" on your business card, but I guarantee you that a majority of your life will be spent selling. A better question might be, are you a good salesman?

Let's start our journey by defining the term. What is selling? If you ask any group of people to define selling you would get a diverse set of answers. As stated earlier, if everyone is a salesman, then the act of selling is ubiquitous. We see it everywhere. From our initial entry into the cognitive world, we have been sold. While you were sitting in a high chair, your mother tried to sell you on the proposition that carrots were good for you. What was her approach? Did you buy it or did you reject the sale? Did you eat those carrots or spit them out?

A sales transaction was taking place, and who would have guessed. It's been that way as long as you've been alive. You are constantly being sold, and you are continually selling. You may not label it "selling," but it is. Call it what you want, here's a fact. If you are trying to get someone else to give you what you want, you are selling. If you succeed more than you fail, you may be a good salesman.

Selling is human interaction manifesting itself in some form. No sales transaction has ever taken place that didn't involve two or more people. It seems logical to me that if we are trying to get another person to give us what we want, it is more likely to happen if the impression we make on them is favorable.

A "normal" person is not knowingly looking to make unfavorable impressions. If they do, it's usually because of ignorance. They weren't aware of the signals they were sending or they were oblivious to the damage their actions caused. The interaction was brief but the negative impact was long lasting. I guess leaving negative impressions won't hurt you if you live in a vacuum, but the fact is you don't. What others think of you is important. How they feel about you will determine how they react to you and their response, good, bad, or indifferent, will have an effect.

THE BASICS

Think about the number of people you encounter in a day. How many individuals do you interface with in the course of living a typical day: ten, twenty, a hundred? Certainly the answer varies, but my guess is, you would be surprised by the number if you ever totaled it.

People are everywhere! We may be able to get away from them on a trek to Nepal, but in our regular day-to-day living there is no escape.

Rational thought would dictate that in those areas where we must interact with another human being, we would want that encounter to be as pleasant as possible. In many cases we want more than just pleasantness. We want something from them.

WHAT THE SMART GUYS SAY

There are a number of experts on the subject of selling that would tell you no sale will be made unless the buyer, in whatever form he exists, perceives that you are fulfilling a need. The process is linear. Exploratory questioning is followed by need fulfillment.

It's interesting that so much emphasis has been placed on procedures that attempt to identify need. I've found in my selling endeavors that determining what a customer needs is usually no more difficult than phrasing the question, "What do you need?" The customer will usually tell you. (Most buyers are not cryptographers or deceivers.) Now, what happens is that you, along with a number of competitors, have that information and the ability to perform. Who gets the order? If you are in the need satisfaction business you might think you do.

I used to believe it, until a few years ago when my vice-president of sales came to me and requested authorization to hire a couple of new salesmen. He went off to college and hired two people. They both looked similar. They dressed well. They were enthusiatic and energetic. We ran them through what we thought was one of the best sales training programs available and inserted them in the market.

Immediately one became a superstar while the other began his slide into the abyss. I didn't understand it. If selling was satisfying a need, why weren't they both successful? They had the resources of a mega-conglomerate behind them. They could satisfy any customer's need. I was perplexed.

At some point later on, I figured it out. When you satisfy a customer's need, all you have done is the same thing as your competition. That's the reason why in every environment, there are multiple competitors. They all buy from the same suppliers at basically the same price and can satisfy any need. If you couldn't satisfy a need you'd be out of business.

I'm not going to tell you that need satisfaction isn't important. It is. It gets you in the ballpark. It allows you to play the game. But if you are going to achieve the highest level of success in the shortest amount of time, you will have to focus on areas that transcend the obvious. I've found the quickest way to build a relationship with someone else is through influence. Gaining influence with a buyer is absolutely critical to the process. When you've gained influence you can dramatically compress the time it takes to build a powerful association.

Let's explore the concept a bit further. The mind is not a calculator. The empirical solutions needed to solve a math problem are seldom appropriate in the decision-making process when human relations are involved. It's been proven that the majority of all decisions are emotional in nature. People act or react in accordance with how they feel about something.

It's estimated that up to 80% of all decisions are made by the right side of the brain, the emotional side. Did you really need those 20 boxes of Girl Scout cookies? How about that $5,000 burial urn for your cat? Emotional decisions are made everywhere.

CAN'T CUT THE MUSTARD BUDDY

Jan Waltz didn't become one of America's top auctioneers by not understanding the concept. Targeting bidders' emotions is the key to his success. Ego, insecurity, self-image, and a host of other emotional catalysts are the psychological tools of the trade. Whether he is complimenting you on your commitment, playing on your insecurity, or feeding your ego, he keeps you in the game. He'll tell you that if you can get a little competition going, rational thought is cast to the wind. A dress will sell for more than a house.

Understanding that people make emotional decisions a majority of the time is highly significant for any salesman trying to capitalize on opportunity. If people are making emotional decisons in favor of empirical decisions and you are providing them with facts, facts, and more facts, it won't be long until you get into trouble.

My experience verifies, it is the salesman who exerts the most influence over the customer that has the greatest level of success. The order is his or hers based upon factors that have nothing to do with need. Satisfying needs will help you sell, but if you want to become a dominant force, you'll have to do more.

Many decisions are devoid of logic or rationality. Understanding the dynamics of a buyer's decision-making process is what Motivational Acceleration is about. In its most complex form, it is nothing more than applying fundamental behavioral science principles to personal relationships to develop them rapidly.

It's a kind of chemical engineering. Do you remember chemistry lab? Nitrogen and calcium when combined elicited no reaction. When you exposed iron to oxygen, you detected something was happening, but the reaction was slow. You had to wait awhile. What happened when water met potassium? You had a kind of spontaneous combustion. The second they encountered each other . . . Bingo . . . you had something.

The human being is a little more complex, and our ability to determine what exactly will happen when two personalities meet is less certain. There are lots of different ways electricity moves through brain matter. Chemistry is an exact science, psychology is not. In our association with other people, their reaction to our actions is less manageable. It comes with how synapses fire. But by understanding some critical components of the relationship building process, we certainly can do much better in determining outcomes.

Motivational Acceleration requires you to be smart. Not intellectually smart, but operationally smart. It demands almost a religious belief that others are the key to your success and happiness in life. If those that surround you are unhappy with you, I can guarantee you, you will be unhappy, less productive, and unfulfilled.

PLEASE DON'T PISTOL WHIP ME MISTER

I worked in New York City for a decade and experienced much of what the Big Apple had to offer, with one exception, I'd never been mugged. I know a lot of people who have though, and having heard countless stories about what transpires, I'm of the opinion there is a school for muggers somewhere on West 91st Street.

Their modus operandi never changes. The attack is swift, aggressive, and highly impersonal. Muggers don't preplan. They go after targets of opportunity. It is always a one-sided affair. The mugger initiates the action, dominates the conversation, and has no concept of quid pro quo.

As I'm writing this, I'm starting to experience déjà vu. I have been mugged! The encounter was identical. The only difference was the mugger didn't carry a gun, he held me hostage with a computer brochure. His M.O. was the same. He approached quickly, did all the talking, and took my money. My reaction was no different than any "muggee." I felt violated and used.

Do you think my analogy is a little far-fetched? I wish it were. Unfortunately there are many parallels between muggers and bad salesmen.

- *Interested in self-gratification.*
- *Abusive.*
- *Oblivious to the consequences of their actions.*
- *Short-term focus.*
- *They will get caught.*

In contrast, Motivationally Accelerated salesmen are the antithesis to what has just been described.

- *Other-centered.*
- *Supportive.*
- *Aware of the impact of their behavior.*
- *Long-term perspective.*
- *Success is never-ending.*

Now having said this I'm continually amazed at how negatively human beings relate to other human beings. It's bad enough if you will never see the individual again, but it takes on overtones of monumental stupidity if you want to influence another individual to help you succeed, and then violate the basic tenets of good behavior.

Look around you. I'm not sure what is causing it but there are a lot of people walking around with attitude problems. Curt, caustic, selfish, and inconsiderate are just a few of the adjectives that describe their actions. Is it any wonder why they may not be achieving what they want from others. Accelerated thinking may not change your attitude but it will enlighten you to the consequences of your behavior.

Are you thoughtful, kind, courteous, obedient, honest, and trustworthy in your relationships? It sounds like the Boy Scout Creed. Do you treat people like you would want to be treated? My goodness, the Golden Rule. You see, when we sell we are interacting with another person who reacts to stimuli much the same way we do. They try to avoid people and situations that engender discomfort. Normal people will gravitate to those they like and avoid those they don't like.

Spectrum of Influence

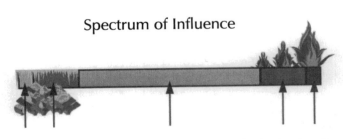

| Impacting | Deceleration | Non-Events – Status Quo | Acceleration | Impacting |

Let's look at a buyer/seller interpersonal relationship model.

In any interpersonal relationship, how one individual relates to another is in large part a result of the degree of influence that exists between them. Influence is necessary in getting another individual to act on something. In normal relationships, influence is gained over an extended period of time. It evolves. In Motivationally Accelerated relationships, it materializes.

THE COLD HARD FACTS

We live in a world of limited resources. Each of us has only so much time, money, and energy, and because of that we have to make choices. The people to whom you are trying to sell have to make choices also. Not everyone gets to win. The winners are usually those individuals who get noticed. The losers live in the shadows. They do what everyone else is doing. Their life is characterized by a never-ending series of Non-Events. They give nothing above the ordinary and therefore get nothing in return.

THE PROCESS

In order to facilitate your understanding of the sales process, let's identify some terms that I think accurately express what is going on in any interpersonal relationship. Right from the start, the moment you encounter another person, you are making an impression on them; physical appearance, enthusiasm, intelligence, and communication all play a part. The individual will internalize what he sees and hears and start to form an opinion about you. If you are average in all areas, the impression you make will be negligible. You will be viewed as a Non-Event. In Wonderland the hopes and wishes of a Non-Event come true, but in the real world being a Non-Event will introduce you to a lot of closed doors.

Non-Events exist for only one reason: the individual doing the selling chooses not to put forth the effort to make the interpersonal interaction memorable.

The majority of all interpersonal interactions are Non-Events. Of the twenty-five people you interfaced with yesterday, how many of them were memorable? If you've taken any sales training courses, you have been taught that a critical component of selling is differentiating yourself from the competition.

If you believe it, then recognize that being average does not set you apart. Most people are average. It's not an indictment. If everyone were outstanding, then outstanding would become average. The majority of us don't fall into that category, but that doesn't mean we can't stand out and standing out is necessary if you are going to impact your customer.

WHO WAS THAT MASKED MAN

When I worked in Manhattan I walked the streets of New York City to keep my waistline in check. On each block I would encounter literally hundreds of people scurrying about. When I returned to my office and thought about the people I'd passed, I couldn't remember anyone. They were just faces in the crowd. Periodically that would change. I would see someone in the distance, six feet, four inches tall, red beret, handlebar mustache, Luchese Ostrich cowboy boots, ivory handled cane, walking a Mastiff. It was a look that got my attention. Had he called out, "Come here buddy I want to talk to you," I would have happily obliged. It's not every day that I get to meet an original.

If you want people to respond to you, you're going to have to get out of the Non-Event. Nothing of any consequence will happen in your selling endeavors if your customer views you as a Non-Event.

Forget the Non-Event, let's create events through Acceleration. Acceleration occurs anytime you make a positive impression on another human being. It involves nothing more than focusing your efforts in areas that turn people on, get them excited, and make them want to have a relationship with you.

If you do a quick review of your recent past with regard to relationships, I'm sure you can recount an experience where the emotional bonding came very quickly. Everything seemed to work. The other person was genuinely interested in what you were presenting and accepted it without resistance. Why? Did you know what you were doing, or was the human chemistry, by accident, just right?

Now reflect back on an encounter where things weren't quite so easy. Communication was strained. Everything was debated, and when the interpersonal interlude was over, you didn't feel very good about it. What happened? I call it Deceleration. Your behavior had a negative impact and lost you influence. Confrontation and rejection are manifestations of decelerating behavior.

In the first situation, you were Accelerating, and in the second, you were Decelerating. In one case, a variety of elements were presented that bonded harmoniously and the psychological union came rapidly—Acceleration. The sale was made. In the other situation, the wrong elements were injected and the relationship deteriorated—Deceleration. No Sale!

I believe salesmen decelerate with customers because of the absence of empirical data showing quantifiable evidence that behavior, good or bad, has a dramatic effect. Customers may not immediately act on their feelings, but over time, the cumulative effect of what the salesman does for them, with them, or to them, will determine the quality of their relationship and ultimately, its success.

Certainly the customer is partly responsible for the treatment she receives. Good communication is characterized by an open expression of how each party feels. If the customer was unhappy with some aspect of how she was being treated, and made the salesman aware of it, "I don't like your rudeness and I'm going to penalize you for it," I suspect the salesman would adjust his behavior immediately. Unfortunately, for the salesman, feelings often aren't expressed until irreparable damage has been done.

Now the scramble is on, and the salesman has to work four times as hard just to get back to a position where the customer might consider him as a resource. Wouldn't it have been easier to do things the right way, up front? It would if you knew what to do and what not to do. Obviously, you would want to do things that score points with your customer and refrain from those activities that lose you points.

Earlier, we said it was difficult to quantify behavior because of all the variables that come into play when two personalities interact. Difficult? Yes. Impossible? No! In order for you to better evaluate where you are in a relationship, being able to keep score is important. We live in a society where scoring determines success or failure. In most cases, the higher the score, the better the performance. We have been conditioned to score and are rewarded for it. Our Motivationally Accelerated program will use a standard of measurement that encourages big numbers.

In some ways, Motivational Acceleration is like playing pinball. Think of your customer as the playing surface and yourself as the pinball. If you are just rolling around and making no contact, there is no score. In certain areas, your contact scores points. In other areas, characterized as danger zones, if you encounter them you lose points and your turn. The object is to maneuver in such a way that you are scoring points while staying out of danger zones. If you are successful, at some point, you will score enough to earn a reward.

In selling, the dynamics are pretty much the same. The object is to score with the customer and when you have hit a threshold of points, a reward will follow. How much is needed? I have no idea. I will tell you, it will vary with every customer you have. There is no set number. There are just too many variables.

History, personality, performance, internal and external influences, and a host of other factors will dictate when and how you score. They will also determine the time frame that governs your ascent from a Non-Event to supplier of choice. That climb can be long and arduous or short and exhilarating. As with any journey, what happens along the way is in large part a result of your preparation up front. I think we should start our preparation with a more detailed discussion of Motivational Acceleration.

CHAPTER 1

MOTIVATIONAL ACCELERATION

Our fears are thieves that steal our confidence and diminish our potential.

MOTIVATIONAL ACCELERATION: *A calculated series of actions that allows you to benchmark the quality of your customer relationships and then implement a program that dramatically improves them at an accelerated pace.*

I think a breakdown of the definition may prove helpful. We said earlier that selling is about getting someone else to give you what you want. As salesmen we need to motivate buyers to act. In order to accomplish more, a salesman needs to accelerate the process. Since we have no desire to waste time, energy, or resources we will only indulge in actions that gain influence.

I have seen many salesmen who were "selling automatons," glorious in their ability to perform a variety of tasks on time within prescribed limits, but miserable failures as salesmen. They never connected with their customers. They looked the part, but for everything they did right, they countered it with something that was wrong. They just didn't know any better. They perceived that action, in and of itself, had worth. And that if you expended resources, success was bound to follow. What they failed to recognize was that if you give more than you get it won't be long before you're bankrupt; physically, emotionally, and financially.

SPARE THE HORSES!

In contrast, a Motivational Accelerator targets the significant and avoids the mundane. In doing so the output/input ratio is highly skewed in his or her favor. For every action there are multiple positive reactions.

Motivational Acceleration dictates that you engage only in actions that get you a payday. No wasted effort is allowed. You save your energy for those activities that get results. Learning how to write an effective thank-you letter will prove far more beneficial than memorizing your price pages. Helping your customer count inventory will score more points than giving the features, advantages, and benefits of your product or service.

Motivational Accelerators understand why targeted thinking and action is necessary. If a salesman can't get to the heart of the issue quickly, operational success remains in abeyance. Nothing is accomplished in "limboland."

Motivational Acceleration prevents that from happening, and it does so through a series of steps that energize the relationship. We calculate because we need to understand the situation. We benchmark so we can measure where we are. We accelerate because we live in a world where fast is better.

Let's get specific. In any sales situation some kind of relationship exists. Its intensity runs the gamut from very positive (lots of success) to very negative (no success). The strength of the relationship is a product of how the individuals feel about each other, and those feelings are not born through immaculate conception. They exist as a result of behavior.

To accelerate a relationship, it is imperative that your actions create a positive perception a majority of the time. Whether you call it common courtesy, etiquette, civility, or good manners, there is no shortage of information on the subject of how to relate to others.

Although we live in an age where the boundaries of acceptable behavior have been stretched, I would suggest that they have not been broken. As a matter of fact, in customer relationships, the parameters are pretty tight. They like you to say "please" and "thank you."

Your customers need to have some criteria by which to evaluate and measure you. If you were the only individual trying to sell them, you might be able to get away with a periodic lapse in performance. The reality is, you are just one of many solicitors looking for an order. It's called competition. You are not only graded on what you are doing, in an absolute sense, you are being evaluated in relation to others.

If you do something the customer doesn't agree with, you drop a notch in her eyes. If your competitor performs in an acceptable manner in that area, he moves up a notch. Get the picture? It's a double whammy, but you can reverse who gets whacked by indulging in accelerating behavior.

ACCELERATOR: Anything that enhances your image in the eyes of the customer.

> *Thoughtfulness, Intelligence, Kindness,*
> *Loyalty, Creativity, Integrity, Appearance,*
> *Generosity, Decisiveness, Enthusiasm,*
> *Credibility, Discipline, Energy, Punctuality,*
> *Commitment, Responsiveness, Cleanliness*

These behavioral traits, when introduced, engender a reciprocal positive reaction. You will gain influence with the person you are trying to sell. In the customer's eyes you are looking better. You're scoring points. Acceleration can be achieved in a thousand different ways. Any action that sends the message to your customer that you are concerned with his well being will score points. How many points you score is up to you.

POSITIVE IMPACTOR: Anything that generates a dramatic change in perception.

Intelligence, Physical Presence, Wealth,
Courage, Speed of Action, Associations

A Positive Impactor is a more robust Accelerator. A Positive Impactor creates an intense reaction. An Accelerator gains ground incrementally while a Positive Impactor is akin to a knockout punch. Save a customer's life. What do you think his response will be the next time you ask him for an order? In what direction will your influence go if you show up on your first sales call with Michael Dell?

A SNAKE'S HEAD FOR PEACE OF MIND

At the start of my professional life I was commissioned a second lieutenant in the U.S. Army. My career path dictated that I attend a number of combat arms schools to insure I was properly trained on my way to becoming an "American fighting man."

Most of the instruction was pretty uneventful until my final qualifying jump in Airborne School. I stood in the ready line, inside a C-130 cargo plane, waiting for the green light to go on, indicating it was time to exit the aircraft. The plan dictated seventeen paratroopers would get out the door in nineteen seconds. Sixteen made it. A second lieutenant, we'll call Dave, didn't. I guess he missed the class on how to hold your static line (the cord that pulls your parachute open), because he let it run under his arm instead of over his shoulder . . . a critical mistake. Dave's static line, upon leaving the airplane, wrapped around his arm and held him to the plane hanging six feet below the jump door. The situation was potentially life threatening but had a happy ending. As Dave flapped in the wind, the pilot brought the plane around whereby the jump master cut the line so Dave could pull the rip cord on his reserve parachute. Dave hit the ground a little embarrassed but pretty much intact.

Three weeks later, I entered Ranger School. So did Dave. Described as the most brutal military training in the world, it appears the program exists for only one reason, physical and mental abuse. Ranger instructors are legendary in their ability to pour sulfuric acid on open wounds. I remember our first formation. We were 220 strong, and in the eyes of the cadre, fresh meat. None fresher than Dave. You see due to Dave's exhilarating airborne experience, he came into Ranger School a known commodity. I'm not sure how long our initial orientation took, but it seemed like 90% of it involved verbally assaulting Dave.

As a matter of fact, every day we had "attack Dave time." In a program that was virtually 24 hours per day for 63 straight days, there was no escape. After three weeks, the class had grown weary of hearing about Dave. I know he felt even worse and that's when I found out Dave was a salesman. He understood impacting and timing.

The sale? Convince the instructors to leave him alone. I remember it as vividly as if it happened last week. We had just finished the Camp Darby skill training phase of the program and were preparing to move on to the mountain phase. We were pulled together for a survival class. One part of the instruction involved learning how to live off the land. We were shown what plants and animals were a good food source and how to prepare them. Killing a variety of creatures in front of the candidates punctuated the point that death and blood were an ever present reality of Ranger life.

The coup de grace of the experience mandated the termination of a giant black snake. As the instructor pulled the reptile from the canvas bag, its serpentine tongue lashed out while it coiled around the instructor's arm. He unsheathed his Ranger utility knife as Blackie awaited his trip to snake heaven. "Wait!", came a scream from the back of the class. "I want to kill that mother . . !" We all turned to find Dave standing with a crazed look in his eyes. "It's yours," said the instructor. Rangers like aggressive behavior. Dave walked up, through a chorus of oohs and aahs, and grabbed the snake and knife. He stood there for a couple seconds, threw the knife down and aggressively inserted the snake's head into his mouth. He had a plan, but unlike Motivational Accelerators, he hadn't done his homework.

Snakeskin is extremely tough. His front teeth were biting ferociously, but making no progress. The oohs and aahs quickly turned to ughs as the snake wrapped itself around Dave's neck.

Failure hadn't been part of the plan. A Postitive Impactor was quickly turning into Deceleration and you could see the look of fear in his eyes. God only knows what was going through his mind. Whatever his doubts, he now had such an adrenaline rush that nothing would stop him. He moved the head to the side of his mouth and chewed it to pieces. As he pulled the headless snake from his mouth, Dave received a standing ovation. We never heard about his parachute jump again. Dave had closed the sale.

Note: For years, as a way of exhibiting machismo, Rangers have bitten the heads off chickens. Chickens heads come off very easily.

The inverse of Acceleration is Deceleration. Instead of scoring points through actions viewed favorably by the customer, Deceleration occurs when negative behavior presents itself. The customer has no desire to grow the relationship. He wants out of it.

DECELERATOR: An action that diminishes your image in the eyes of the customer.

> *Rudeness, Lethargy, Thoughtlessness, Ignorance, Sarcasm, Arrogance, Pomposity, Aloofness, Myopia, Disinterest, Tardiness, Laziness, Deceit*

The exhibition of any one of these traits will cost you and if you indulge regularly in decelerating behavior, your chances of establishing a meaningful partnership are virtually nonexistent.

This concept is lost on many of the telemarketers who annoy each of us. I don't know who is providing the script, but telling people at the beginning of a conversation that you are not trying to sell them something, when in fact you are, is a lie. When a relationship is founded on deceit only one thing should happen. Click. A much better approach would be to start the conversation off with an apology and a thank you. Time is precious, and when you take some from someone else you should thank him or her for it. Your awareness and sensitivity will score.

There are lots of ways to decelerate a relationship.

DECELERATING ACTIONS

Deceleration occurs anytime your performance impacts the customer negatively. Listed below are twenty actions that will have a deleterious effect on your relationship with your customer.

DECELERATORS

■ **Not returning your customer's phone calls promptly.**
People make phone calls for a reason. In many instances they are looking for a response to something that concerns them. When you don't return phone calls promptly, you are making a statement that their concerns are not a high priority with you. So many salesmen are so bad at returning phone calls quickly; if you do you will stand out. If you don't, the customer will find a salesman who will and give him your opportunities.

■ **Making disparaging comments to your customer about your competition.**
Your customer is buying from your competition for a reason! If they were bad, they probably wouldn't be a supplier. When you put down a competitor, you are putting down your customer. The customer makes a conscious decision to give business to someone else. Earn the business on your strength, not someone else's weakness. Weak salesmen focus on what others can't do rather than what they can do.

■ **Keeping your customer waiting.**
Time is life's most precious commodity. No one has a right to take it from someone else. Be a fanatic about being on time and you will gain a reputation. Take time away from your customer, and he will most certainly take his time away from you. Your time is his, but if you think the inverse is true, think again.

■ **Dropping by without an appointment.**
If something is important enough to see your customer about, it only makes sense you alert her to a visit. She can then schedule you when it's best for her. When you just drop by, you stand a

good chance of disrupting her day. If she then has to accommodate you because you are there, you'll lose points.

■ **Asking your customer to pick up his portion of a check for food, drink, or entertainment.**
Your customer's orders are your success. Without them you are unemployed. When you ask your customer to pay his way, you are telling him that the relationship is a one-sided affair and it centers around you.

■ **Not responding immediately to a customer's request.**
When you respond slowly you send many messages.

1. You don't value the input.

2. You're lazy.

3. You're preoccupied.

4. You're incompetent.

5. You are not a valuable resource.

Get on top of things quickly, and stay on them until the customer is satisfied with your response. He may not be happy with your answer, but if your response is swift, he will continue to call you.

■ **Giving your customer inaccurate information.**
Successful operations require good intelligence. If you provide bad information, you damage your customer's ability to perform and your credibility. Very quickly, you will become worthless.

■ **Being inconsistent in your selling methods.**
There is something about the human being that yearns for consistency. Inconsistency catapults situations into turmoil. In order to develop a plan, people need to know what they can count on. They will almost always gravitate to salesmen and situations that are predictable.

■ **Complaining to the customer when things don't go your way.**
Generally, customers make decisions that are in their best interest. Hopefully, many of those decisions will favor you, but if they

don't, complaining about them creates a perception that you are more concerned with your well being than with theirs.

■ **Arguing with your customer.**
When you argue with a customer, you are telling her you know more about the issue than she does. You may, but I would suggest you give what information you have on the subject without judgmental overtones. Upsetting the person who pays your mortgage will cost you points. It's her business, and she has a right to run it how she chooses.

■ **Asking for an order before you've performed.**
In fairy tales you get something for nothing. In selling, performing for the customer is a prerequisite for future success. Asking for business before you've earned it says you are naive, greedy, and ignorant of the dynamics of selling. Insure you have held up your end of the contract. Then, when your customer gives you business, which he will probably take from someone else, he will feel good about it.

■ **Not thanking your customer, on a regular basis, for business he is giving you.**
No one wants to be taken for granted.

■ **Showing a lack of self-discipline in your customer's presence.**
Self-discipline is a highly admired trait. Lack of it creates a perception that situations can get the better of you. Customers like to do business with salesmen who are capable of controlling their environment. Excess, in any form, decelerates relationships.

■ **Showing displeasure when you do something for your customer that is not in your best interest.**
Give and take is the nature of selling. Not every situation will favor you. If the relationship is healthy, the pendulum will always swing back. The image you should convey is: whatever is good for your customer, ultimately, is good for you.

■ **Not communicating regularly with your customer about everything that impacts the relationship.**

Salesmen are the communication link between their company and the customer. Good decisions cannot be made without timely, accurate information. Without a salesman's input, a customer's operation will experience paralysis. If you are not inputting intelligence, your customer will find an alternate source.

■ **Telling your customer how to run his business.**

In relating to your customer, never "tell" him anything. Respond to his requests for assistance, or suggest alternatives to his present mode of operation, but let him make the decision on how to run his business. I've found more often than not, ownership engenders a sensitivity about decision making that is not conducive to instructional input.

■ **Giving in to your customer too quickly on issues that are important to you and your company.**

Being a valuable resource to your customer means having knowledge in areas that transcend your customer's frame of reference. Backing down quickly on issues creates a perception that your knowledge has little worth, or your reluctance to take a stand characterizes you as spineless. In either case, you lose.

■ **Not understanding your customer's business.**

In order to provide the kind of support your customer needs to be successful, you must have an in-depth knowledge of his business. Without it, your attempts to help will be off target and of little value.

■ **Ignoring any customer employee.**

You never know what role a person plays in an organization. Treat everyone with respect and you won't have to worry that your efforts will be undermined by someone you ignored when he surfaces as a key player. Treat everyone with consideration, because it's the right thing to do.

■ **Taking your customer for granted.**
There will always be plenty of competitors who will be happy to make your customer feel special. If you take him for granted, it's only a matter of time before you are on the outside looking in.

Timing has a lot to do with a salesman's success. The world we live in is becoming a pretty complex place and most people have a lot on their mind. Being able to recognize when someone is mentally with you or distracted is key to making an effective sales presentation. Trying to sell someone when the timing is wrong will get you nothing. In some instances due to a lack of sensitivity you will decelerate rapidly.

WAIT YOUR TURN

Not long ago, while in Napa Valley for a meeting I decided to eat at one of the most popular restaurants in the area, La Travigne. It's understood that if you want to enjoy the ambiance and gourmet treats of this restaurant, a reservation should be made far in advance. Would they take me on a moment's notice? Only if I employed Motivational Acceleration.

As expected the reservationist greeted my phone call with disdain. While she didn't specifically say it, the interpretation was clear. How dare you call us on this short notice. Get Lost! My wife heard the conversation and inquired where would we eat. I responded, La Travigne.

When we showed up the place was packed. I could see that the owner, who normally seats you, was distracted. It was no time to make my pitch. While my wife and I stood there, numerous couples entered and requested a table. Each was summarily dismissed. We waited approximately fifteen minutes until the activity subsided and I could see the owner had a more relaxed look on his face. I approached quickly, delivered three compliments, and stated that I was one of his biggest fans. I was such a fan that I recommended his restaurant to people around the world. My wife and I were in the area and I wanted to expose her to a great experience. Was there any possibility of getting a meal? We would be happy to eat in the kitchen. I explained I didn't expect him to accommodate my request on such short notice, but I had to ask.

Because the timing was right, he had the opportunity to size me up. Standing in front of him was a fan and promoter who was also considerate and sensitive to restaurant protocol. His reaction came quickly; he pulled a small table from a back room and invited us to participate in the festivities. The complimentary bottle of wine was unnecessary.

Sales success is seldom accomplished by brute force. Finesse always works better. When you exhibit behavior that targets the interest of others and properly time your delivery, results can come quickly. Attempting to force the issue will not only fail but will leave a lasting negative impression.

Some individuals are so ignorant of the dynamics that govern interpersonal associations, they will attempt to close a sale even when they have indulged in Negative Impacting. They fail to recognize that there are certain actions that are so disdained, that no one wants an association with the perpetrator. Call it a customer's "Hot Button." When it's triggered, something immediate and highly negative happens. No Sale!

Negative Impactors:
Cowardice, Stupidity, Dishonesty, Greed

PREPARE FOR SURPRISES

If you're evaluating my list of Accelerators, Decelerators, and Impactors, you might disagree with my categorization. For you, wealth is not a Positive Impactor, it's a Decelerator. Every wealthy person you've known was a jerk. Dishonesty is not a Negative Impactor. The environment in which you operate is full of dishonest people, so it's nothing worse than a Decelerator.

I've been surprised a number of times in my selling career by overestimating or underestimating the power of my ammunition. Usually

SELLING

it occurred because I hadn't done
enough information available to e
came quickly and I didn't leave w
every now and then, I fell into ser

immediate ex
experience
part of a
set me
Bh
t

AN ALTERNATIVE TO MANSLAU

A number of years ago, I had t
sales manager at International Paper Co.
ing my responsibilities, I asked to accompany one of my
resentatives on a sales call to an account she had just lost. (The names
have been changed to protect the guilty.)

She gave me a briefing on the situation, told me the company was
our worst customer, and our potential for turning the account around
was zero. We landed in Detroit, rented a car, and headed for the
account. As we got closer, I could see that my sales rep was becoming visibly agitated by the thought of confronting two honor gradu-
ates of the "Ivan the Terrible School of Purchasing."

It disturbed me to watch her emotional transformation. I recognized
the fear in her face and couldn't believe it. How bad could this customer be? The sign on the roof gave me some indication. It must
have been used in a past Super Bowl. The art deco monstrosity read,
"World Headquarters." In that I knew it was a single-location company, it appeared ego had gotten the best of the company. Little did
I know how much.

We sat in the lobby for an hour. The customer was sending me a
message. Finally, the Vice President of Operations, Mike Bhutto, sum-
moned us. We walked into his smoke-filled, dimly lit gymnasium of
an office, and there he sat behind a desk that approximated the size
of our rental car. Everything about him disgusted me. I wanted to
carry on the conversation from outside his office door, but two
wooden chairs were placed strategically in front of him.

We sat down and as he gazed at us, a kind of crazed look materialized on his face. Initially I thought he had eaten a bad burrito. His

plosion indicated it was something else. I had never
a more vitriolic tirade. This is a joke, I thought. It's all
regional initiation for the new manager. My sales rep had
up. It didn't take long to realize she hadn't, and I recognized
to had some serious emotional problems. His one-sided dia-
be took everyone hostage; my sales representative, my company,
and I were all guilty of the problems they were experiencing. We
were an anathema and they would never do business with us again.
Lawsuits were imminent.

He hadn't come up for air and as he continued, I had time to think
about my response. His all encompassing abuse went beyond reason, so I soon found myself getting very emotional. My blood pressure skyrocketed and I started to reflect back on my years as an Army
Ranger. I knew at least ten ways to kill someone. Which one would
I use on Bhutto? The business no longer mattered. Hand grenades,
M-16's, Claymores, and C-4 flashed in front of my eyes. If he stopped
to catch his breath, I would launch a counter offensive. I didn't care
if I went to jail.

Miraculously, I came to my senses. I wasn't a sales representative calling on the account. My business card said sales manager. I had to
set an example. I would keep my cool. To this day, I don't know
where my response to Bhutto's attack came from. I hadn't read Tony
Parinello's *Selling to Vito*, and in many ways, still flew by the seat of
my pants.

From out of nowhere a voice in my head told me to compliment
him. I rejected the thought but when I opened my mouth the words
flowed forth. "Mike, let me commend you for saying what's on your
mind. It's individuals with backbone that force suppliers to be better. Most people in dealing with a five billion dollar company would
be afraid to speak their mind." After I had uttered those words, I
could not believe they came from me. The Patron Saint of Selling
obviously wanted my career to continue.

I waited for his response. It seemed like an eternity. He must have
been in shock. You could see him psychologically processing my comment. His face started to take on a softer look. His response, his

incredible response was, "Steve, it's not that bad." It was awestruck! It had worked. I couldn't believe my ears. Something profoundly significant had just occurred and I didn't know why. Subsequent experience has taught me why. The placement of a well timed, well articulated compliment is a powerful relationship building tool.

About that time, Joe Flynn, the owner, entered the office. He physically wasn't as intimidating as Bhutto, but he had a look in his eye that was no less menacing. They had honed their Bad Cop, Bad Cop routine to a razor's edge. It was attack time for Flynn.

I wasn't going to wait. I learned in the Rangers to take the offensive. Should I pull out my bayonet? No, I decided instead to pull out another compliment. Bhutto introduced us, and as he and Flynn exchanged comments, Bhutto gave him a look that I interpreted as saying, "This guy is okay."

I seized the opportunity. Here it comes. "Joe, I want to commend you on your choice of Vice President of Operations. Mike has forced us to do things that run counter to standard operating procedures. He's tough, but he's fair." What nonsense. I was gagging as I said it but I'd received such a favorable response from my first compliment that I wanted to roll the dice again.

It worked! Flynn's ego had been stroked. His decision had put Bhutto in that position. Wasn't he a smart guy. My comment also scored with Bhutto. Complimenting him in front of the guy who paid his salary did wonders for our relationship. He now saw me as an ally. It didn't take long after that to get a consensus that maybe our two companies could work together. We followed up on a number of issues they presented and things were back on track shortly thereafter. To this day, thousands of sales calls later, my day in Detroit stands as one of my proudest sales moments. It all started with a compliment.

I now use the compliment as a means of starting every relationship. It's as easy as breathing. There is always something that can be complimented. Clothing, appearance, disposition, interests, attitude, and approach are all targets of opportunity. You'll find as you compliment people you will break down the defensive barriers that many individuals possess. I've never seen anybody react negatively to a compliment.

Spend enough time on your investigative preplan, and your use of Accelerating actions will hit pay dirt. Remember that discussion on chemistry and psychology? There is variability in how people view things, and because of that, we will never be able to pinpoint precisely where we are on the Spectrum of Influence. It doesn't matter! What we are concerned with is the trend: is it up or down? Are we bonding with our customer or are our actions tearing the relationship apart? There is no optimum strategic selling plan—an optimal course of action works just fine.

SLIDE RULES AREN'T NECESSARY

We stated earlier that it is difficult to measure behavior in numerical terms, but not impossible. If we are going to decipher where we are in the relationship, we must, as best we can, quantify the situation. It's important to turn human activity into a form that is measurable. If we don't, it's difficult to see where we stand. In order to do that, a simple model has been created that allows you to track and grade your actions. It is nothing more than a scorecard, and your ability to gain or lose points comes directly from your use of Accelerators, Positive Impactors, Decelerators, and Negative Impactors.

If we are going to establish our position in the relationship, we need to measure our actions. I can think of no better way of measuring our performance than using the Base Ten numbering system. But instead of using all ten numbers, we will use only two—the numbers five and ten.

Don't get turned off by this simple approach. Not everything needs to be complicated. Others use it also. Computers operate on a similar principle. The speed at which they process information is a direct result of their use of the Binary System of numeration. They also use only two numbers, zero and one.

We could try to be more accurate by incorporating smaller increments of measurement, but it would only complicate the issue without providing any better data. You see, as I have stated, we aren't ever exactly sure the absolute impact our actions have, but it's my experience that individuals can tell, with some certainty, whether their behavior is being viewed positively or negatively.

The signals are everywhere. Does the customer appear pleased to see you? Does he engage in extended conversations or are his answers curt and icy? Does he return your phone calls? Has he done anything nice for you lately? Are you included or excluded in his program? Is he confrontational or agreeable?

Each action is a direct result of how the customer views your relationship. If you've been Accelerating, scoring points, customer interaction is a pleasurable experience. On the other hand, if Deceleration has been the principle component of your selling style, you're in trouble. How much trouble? You can figure it out using a Sales Acceleration Log (SAL).

SAL is nothing more than a tool that helps you keep a record of your behavior. As I've stated, we want to quantify what we do so we can measure it. When using SAL, there are four levels of scoring that will register—two positives and two negatives. Accelerators carry a weight of +5, Positive Impactors +10, Decelerators -5, and Negative Impactors -10. You need to establish a time frame for your actions. Did they occur over a week, a month, or a year?

Obviously, the longer the time between actions, the more diluted they become. Accelerators, over time, turn into Non-Events. Now that we've established these ground rules, let's take a look at how your influence might grow at an account.

To keep things simple, we will always start the exercise with no score, 0. When you've concluded the scoring, you can then add to or subtract from a previous total. Recognize that the score we achieve from SAL has no other purpose than to determine a numerical value so we can plot it on the Spectrum of Influence. The running total determines whether you are Accelerating or Decelerating. Have we done enough to transcend the Non-Event and move forward or are our actions having a negative impact?

Acceleration and Deceleration occur in a variety of ways. What you think are insignificant actions may not be. There are lots of ways to gain or lose points.

SALES ACCELERATION LOG (SAL)				
DECELERATORS	–	BAL	+	ACCELERATORS
Did not follow up on a request	–5	0	+5	Brought your customer a gift
Showed up late for a presentation	–5	+5	+10	Helped a daughter get an interview
Argued over a pricing issue	–5	+5	+5	Bought lunch after a big order
Didn't return a phone call	–5	+5	+5	Helped them count inventory
		+10	+5	Sent them an article on something
		+15	+5	Helped an employee with his job
		+20	+5	Wrote a letter commending them
Totals	**–20**	**+60**	**+40**	

DECELERATION

ACTION	SCORE
1. We don't call the customer for an appointment, we just drop by.	−5
2. Our appearance is a little rough.	−5
3. We have no sales promotion tools, no information documents.	−5
4. We have other things to do so we're impatient.	−5
5. Our grammar isn't proper.	−5
6. We are asked a question and have no answer.	−5
7. We tell the customer we will get back with an answer that afternoon and it takes two days.	−5
8. We know the answer will not please the customer so we lie to him.*	−10
	−45

* An old adage expresses it very well: Lose your wealth, you've lost nothing. Lose your health, you've lost something. Lose your credibility, you've lost everything!

Could we have done it differently? Let's see.

ACCELERATION	
ACTION	SCORE
1. We show courtesy by calling for an appointment.	+5
2. We always dress for success.	+5
3. We never go anywhere without support material.	+5
4. We always show patience because customers are the key to success.	+5
5. We've developed excellent written and verbal skills.	+5
6. We don't have the answer but we make a call on the spot to get it.	+5
7. We have someone else call the customer to insure he understood what he was told.	+5
8. We never lie to our customer. The truth, no matter how bad, is always better.	+5
	+40

Can you see how being able to measure behavior helps take the subjectivity out of your opinion on where you stand? In the first example, you are in a Decelerating mode. In the second, you are in Acceleration. You still may be a long way from an order, but the trend is up. Your score determines you are doing the right things.

We could come up with another hundred scenarios and the book would weigh a lot more, but the fundamentals wouldn't change. In all selling activities, there are right and wrong ways to do things.

Certainly the degree to which they are right or wrong, is in large part due to how your customer views them. What are his fears, values, past experiences, and objectives? All will play a part in how he reacts.

Recognize also that moving up the Spectrum of Influence is a relative state of affairs. You have competition. You will be awarded points not only on an absolute basis but also on a relative basis. How do your actions stack up against the competition?

MORE ESCARGOT PLEASE

Recently I was sitting at my desk when the phone rang and a "hot shot" in the financial services industry told me he had just completed reading an article I had written. He continued by saying he had employed the program I suggested for his entire selling career and that I had taught him nothing new with one exception: How relativity impacts the acceleration of a relationship. A brief story followed.

He had identified a business tycoon who needed a money manager. As part of his accelerating program he flew the individual and his wife to New York City to attend the U.S. Open tennis tournament. He thought his creative Positive Impactor would open the relationship. The call never came. Four months later he found out a viable competitor had flown the tycoon and his wife to Paris for a week. The U.S. Open versus dinner and bowling is a Positive Impactor. The U.S. Open versus champagne at the Eiffel Tower is a Non-Event.

THE FRIENDSHIP TRAP

When thinking about accelerating a relationship, many a salesman has gotten into trouble because his focus is on building new and prosperous relationships. He forgets that his present relationships need to be accelerated also. It's hard to move ahead if you acquire a new customer but lose an old one. Two steps forward and two steps back will keep you in the Non-Event forever. Let's look at an event in the SAL to see how this might happen.

ACTION

We don't call our customer for an appointment; we just drop by.

On the surface it would appear that there is nothing wrong with this approach. We've been calling on the account for years and our customer is our friend. He or she doesn't mind if we just show up. You're probably right. You won't be docked any points for lack of courtesy but you also won't be given any points. Your action is a Non-Event. You score zero.

A Motivationally Accelerating competitor makes that courtesy call. She scores five. In what other areas have you taken your customer for granted because of friendship? Where else has your competitor scored while you played the role of Non-Event? Now multiply that over an extended period of time. It all adds up and when it does the outcome is predictable. One day you show up and your business has been given to someone else. While you were being friendly, your competitor knocked your socks off. It is a relative world we live in.

DON'T WASTE AMMUNITION

You don't want to jump too quickly in sizing up your target. Human beings are complex animals. More often than not, my first impression of someone is usually wrong, and if not wrong, incomplete. But with time and interaction, the substantive aspects of their personality come to the forefront.

Motivational Acceleration reduces wasted effort. Although it involves speed, it places a high priority on patience and planning. Acceleration, in many ways, is analogous to taking a trip. If you get in your car and just start driving, there is a chance you will take some wrong turns and possibly get lost. Wasted time. Wasted energy. If you buy a map and read it, whatever the initial cost in time and money it will certainly be repaid in the course of your travel.

Motivational Accelerators know lots of ways to get things done. Great Accelerators are like magicians. As with any magic show, they need to know their audience's level of expectation. If they came to see a tiger disappear, they won't be satisfied with seeing a pigeon pulled from a hat. Understanding your customer is a necessity.

Over the years, I have probably given a thousand speeches. When I first started, I would prepare a speech based primarily on what I wanted to say. With experience I now speak on what I believe the audience wants to hear. The reaction is always better. The same holds true when trying to sell someone. The customer has certain feelings about the natural order of things. You are part of that order and need to adjust your behavior accordingly. If you are going to Accelerate, being in sync with a buyer's view is important.

I've found that most people are not an open book and a little analysis is required to discover what makes them tick. Therefore, Motivational Acceleration consists of five operational components:

- *Research*
- *Observation*
- *Experimentation*
- *Identification*
- *Implementation*

All activities focus on the customer. We Research to gather information about them. Observation is needed to see if our intelligence is confirmed by their actions. Experimentation tests our hypotheses. Identification labels our target and mandates a certain type of ammunition. Implementation involves all of those customer-directed actions that motivate them to play with us.

The process is iterative by nature. To move ahead we must test, evaluate, readjust, and implement. With experience, the time between testing and implementing is shortened. We acquire a feel for what will work and what won't.

We recognize that there are cause and effect relationships between actions. Patterns of activity become clear and responses predictable. We score like a pinball wizard. Influencing others becomes child's play. Well, not quite. You see, none of this happens by just talking or thinking about it. It requires, and I'll say it again, effort on your part. You must act!

I know, if you could be guaranteed that a Motivationally Accelerated selling program would give you much of what you want in life, you'd start it today. Effort would be no obstacle. Does your reluctance to get going involve trust? It wouldn't surprise me. How many miracle cures have there been? Are you impatient for results? I wanted everything yesterday, too.

There was nobody more impatient than I was twenty years ago. I was in a hurry to succeed and in the absence of guarantees and my own ignorance, when I didn't see signs of immediate success I got bored or frustrated and moved on. I knew nothing about Motivational Acceleration. I didn't realize I needed to be out of the Non-Event before anything of any consequence was going to happen with my customer.

I knew I was well received, but I wasn't aware I was thirty points shy of Acceleration. Six accelerators would have done it. One day's effort. The brass ring was within my grasp.

WHAT DO POPCORN AND SELLING HAVE IN COMMON?

Records reflect that popcorn was introduced by an Indian named Quadequina at the first Thanksgiving in 1632. I knew it wasn't in the Middle Ages. There were just too many things going on. You never knew when you were going to have to go off to war. It could be any minute.

You see, when you put corn kernels in a pan and put a fire under them, initially, nothing happens. They just sit there. Jiggle them around and still, by all external appearances, they look moribund, dead to the world. We know they aren't. Inside a reaction is taking place. The heat being applied is having an effect. We keep at it because we know, either through experience or instruction, that at some point the temperature of the corn will reach a level that requires it to pop.

As you know, all the corn does not pop at once because there is variability among kernels. (Some never pop.) But, once the popping starts, in a very short time frame, you have it . . . a bowl of popcorn.

In selling, the course of events is almost identical to popping corn. Customers are sitting there waiting to be energized. Great customers are not born, they are created. It is the salesman's job to apply enough heat to get the process started.

Initially, as Accelerators and Positive Impactors are introduced, it may appear like nothing is happening. There is no evidence the customer is going to open the relationship. In their present state, their value is marginal, but if you can get them to pop, the main feature will be a lot more enjoyable. In selling and popping corn, success is a function of time.

Although the situation looks dormant, growth is occurring. You may have thought those corn kernels didn't change until the actual pop, but in fact they had. They began to swell right from the start.

Acceleration with another person occurs the same way. Initially the changes are very subtle. He drops you a note. He tells you a joke. You're invited into his office. He is in no hurry to finish the conversation. He suggests you get a beer. He thanks you for your time. You may not have the order but the direction of the relationship is north. Once you start to see a change, shift into a higher gear. This is not the time to be conservative. You're making an impact with your actions and now you need to stir up the situation.

INTERPRET THIS

A young lady approached me after a speech in Los Angeles desirous of discussing the correlation between selling and popping corn. She told me she had been calling on an account for almost year but had seen very little in the way of tangible success. The relationship with her buyer was cordial and the environment had grown increasingly friendly but orders had not followed.

One day, the owner invited her into his office. In that she had had few conversations with him and never been in the executive sanctum it came as a surprise. Shortly into the conversation he began talking about a vasectomy reversal. Sexual harassment, she thought? No, a medical procedure you would not be discussing with a stranger, she concluded. The relationship had obviously moved farther along than she'd thought. Was the corn about to pop?

Her subsequent purchase of a bottle of Dom Perignon and accompanying note wishing him and his wife good luck helped insure it would. A week later a competitor's relationship was given to her. The signs were obvious. She interpreted them correctly and made an Accelerating move. A Non-accelerator would have called an attorney.

Unfortunately for many salesmen, their selling approach is analogous to fishing with a drift net. They just hang around hoping they will catch something. Because they have no recipe for success, they are never really sure if their actions are hitting the mark. They hope that what they are doing is working, but in the absence of concrete feedback an operational insecurity begins to grow. Now they are looking for any excuse to bail out. They want to find an easier target.

I guess they thought the lock that secures the door to the customer's heart could be opened with a church key. They were misinformed! There is no lock. In my twenty-five years of professional selling, I can't recall a situation where anyone raised his hand and said, "Stop, I don't want to hear about a better situation."

The reason is obvious. Intelligent people recognize that in virtually all things, there are better alternatives, and one way of finding out about them is through human interaction. Hearing someone else's story can be highly informative and profitable. People want to be sold, but they will decide who sells them.

Your challenge is not unlike getting through a maze. There is an entry and exit. Successful navigation involves nothing more than finding the correct path. With proper instruction, you will enter and exit quickly. You know that many of the paths that present themselves lead to nowhere. You will not take them. Time, effort, and resources will be saved.

The inverse is, you've been given no guidance. Every choice is an experiment, a guess. Every path is taken to its unproductive end. Energy is wasted. A wrong turn and you are back where you started, frustrated and worn out. Quitting looks like an inviting option to starting over. There must be a better way.

CHAPTER 2

KNOW YOUR BUSINESS

The two laziest words I know are "what if."

In 1960, when ACME High School played their crosstown rival in football, if you asked who was playing linebacker for ACME, the answer would not have been Bill Gates. If you scanned the stadium to see who was cheering for the home team, in all probability Bill's mug would not have been present. It wasn't that Bill didn't have an interest in sports, it just took a back seat to more important activities.

He understood whatever athletic prowess he achieved in his youth would diminish with age. He was interested in investing his energy in something that would grow stronger with time . . . Knowledge.

Bill doesn't look like Brad Pitt and for all I know he moves like a handcuffed hippopotamus. But, in the Information Age none of that matters. Being able to play on the world stage is a function of smarts, not physical capability. All-State athletes are forgotten after the senior prom; rocket scientists go into the history books.

Stupid went out with the dinosaurs and dumb will get you a job as an assistant janitor. The world is being run by brain power. "Nerd" has taken on celebrity status, which creates a wonderfully just circumstance. It doesn't matter that genetics slam dunked you when it came to appearance because in the long run what you know always wins out over how you look.

THERE IS NO SUBSTITUTE FOR KNOWLEDGE!

From the moment you walk through a customer's door, you are being evaluated and compared. Evaluated on what you bring to the relationship, as well as compared to your competition, past and present.

Failure on your part to grasp the essentials of the business relationship relegates you to second-class citizenship. Any decision maker who runs a successful enterprise expects the salesman who gets a disproportionate share of his business to be a major contributor in the area of intelligence. Timely, accurate information is the price of admission.

For those of you who have an empirical bent, let me express it mathematically: C2FKC4. A simple formula that states that your Competence and Confidence as a salesman is a Function of the Knowledge of your Capabilities, the Customer, your Company, and the Competition.

When was the last time you did an analysis of the strengths and weaknesses of your toughest competitor. How good are they? Do they have an Achilles heel? Knowledge can eliminate the fear generated by your competitor's public relations machine. Bigger, faster, tougher, smarter might be all hype. When you put them under a microscope you may find that they are covered with warts. But, until you've done some research you won't be able to develop an effective strategic selling plan. Any road warrior will tell you, it is imperative that you identify where the soft spot lies. Is your competitor weak on customer service, consistency, turnaround, or pricing?

When you juxtapose your strength against their weakness the competitive gap looks wider. Cognitive dissonance can be created, which you can capitalize on. Buyers who make emotional decisions have been known to react quickly when they perceive a service inbalance.

THERE'S GOLD IN THEM HILLS

Because everyone needs to be knowledgeable, the payday for making people more informed is monumental. Think about it. Due to an association with you, a buyer is more capable of doing her job, or some other job for that matter. Doesn't it seem logical that the buyer would reward you for enhancing her ability to capitalize on the issues, threats, opportunities, and challenges that confront her? What if you enhanced her personal life too. Any score there?

Some salesmen don't think so. If you chronicled their entire selling career, you would find that it never transcended the product or service. What they failed to recognize was that the product and service was about them and their company. When a purchase was made, they benefited and their company benefited. So no score.

Does bringing knowledge into a relationship sound like a lot of work? It might have been in the Agrarian Age, but in today's environment information is everywhere. Get on the Internet and in one hour you can download enough material to accelerate relationships for a decade. How inportant are health-related issues to people? Send an article on Vitamin E and you'll find out.

Are you afraid you might waste time by sending them something they don't need? Don't be. You'll still be rewarded for the effort. Thoughtfulness and consideration will accelerate even the hardest heart.

A LAST GASP

I started my selling career in the paper industry with International Paper Company. As the new guy on the block I was given a potpourri of bum accounts and told to "make it happen." As a novice, thirty days out of the army with no sales training, I went to my local bookstore to seek advice. A variety of experts told me to learn the features, advantages, and benefits of my product and service and attack. Sounded like good advice. I identified the worst performing account in the region and decided I would start there. The head honcho was a gentleman by the name of Tom Keefe. He had a reputation for being unbelievably obstinate and his dislike (for good reasons) for International Paper Company bordered on hatred. For six months I attempted to get an appointment with him. "Not a chance," I was told very directly.

I did call on the buyers at the account but due to Tom's influence I had no success. However, in the course of my conversations with underlings, I found out that Tom was liked by his employees, respected by his peers, and had an insatiable interest in everything. His Bonsai tree collection was said to be world class. I'd never heard of a monster growing little trees. Could it be that under that titanium exterior was actually a human being? Two days later I found out.

While killing time at a mall waiting for an appointment, I happened to walk by a bookstore. In the window the most beautiful book on Bonsai trees ever created was showcased. The price made me choke. Tom Keefe hadn't earned a comic book much less this masterpiece. I bought it and mailed it that day with an accompanying note. I figured I had nothing to lose.

> Dear Tom,
>
> I found this book at a flea market for a penny. You're worth at least that much to me. In reading it, I noticed there is a direct correlation between the size of Bonsai trees and the orders you give International Paper. Enjoy.

His response was swift. The day he received my gift of knowledge I was called and asked if I would meet him for lunch. It was the start of one of the most prosperous relationships in my selling career. What made it happen? You tell me.

THE KING OF NORTH

Seymour Surnow understands the concept completely. His rise to superstardom began the moment he took on the role of "Library of Congress" for the neighborhood.

As the head of the Surnow Group of realtors in Washington Depot, Connecticut, he sells real estate to the world's most wealthy and powerful people. He understands that they succeeded by knowing more so providing more information is at the crux of his accelerating program. Not only does he inform you about everything that has to do with your purchase, he provides a panoply of insightful material that enhances your entire living experience. If you want to know what kind of olive oil they use at Robert and Adrianna Mnuchin's Mayflower Inn you'll find it on page two of his newsletter.

Surnow's approach is not novel, Motivational Accelerators employ the technique everywhere. Linus Cooke, the stockbroker of the year for Smith Barney, delivers an informational cornucopia to his customers that boggles the mind. Much of it is irrelevant to any specific situation but he scores regardless. People appreciate the effort and attention. The message is loud and clear—Linus Cooke is on a quest to find the perfect stock.

Another great thing about knowledge is it's portable. Because you never know when a sales opportunity may present itself, when you have an encyclopedia on your shoulders you are always ready to respond. The difference between success or failure might be an hour.

Today information is so easily acquired only apathy would prevent someone from becoming more informed. Would you want an apathetic saleman as your supplier of choice? Neither does your customer. They are looking for salesmen who can enhance the interpersonal relationship.

If you didn't think you needed to know anything about sports, leisure, food, travel, politics, or the arts, think again. I've never heard anyone complain about a salesman being too interesting. When your customer perceives you have something to offer that transcends the business relationship, he or she will want to spend more time with you. Time is opportunity.

Are your invitations for social interaction rejected? Maybe you need a makeover. Take that black and white personality and turn it into technicolor. Get on the Internet or get on the road.

A RENAISSANCE MAN

Well, not exactly. When I hired him he was an enthusiastic, dedicated, intelligent dud. It wasn't that he was apathetic about acquiring knowledge, it had more to do with circumstance. He came from a small town, went to a small college, worked at small jobs, and had a small family.

The problem was, he now lived in a big city, had a big territory, and called on big buyers at big accounts. When customers engaged him in conversation it never transcended the mundane. You couldn't blame him, his life's experience had been limited.

Day after day he interfaced with the industry big whigs and when the conversation turned to social issues he had little to say. In the absence of knowledge, I could feel his confidence waning. Having an insecure salesman would inhibit my ability to win the war.

The plan materialized quickly. It was time for some international exposure. There is something about riding a gondola in Venice that makes you feel important. I called him into my office and handed him a map of southern Europe. Five cities were circled: Zermatt, Lake Como, Florence, Venice, and Munich. His whirlwind tour would expose him to some of the most beautiful places on earth. I hoped his immersion in some very distinct cultures would round him out.

Having made the swing on numerous occasions, I gave him detailed instructions on where to invest his time to maximize his learning experience. I would give him the days off but he would have pay his own way. He accepted the offer and within a month had completed the adventure.

Shortly thereafter, he and I entertained a California business legend and also the CEO of his biggest account. On a previous dinner I had carried the conversation. On this night I sat back and watched my budding superstar entertain the table. The caterpillar I had sent to the Alps had returned a butterfly. The salesman who got lost in the supermarket was now a travel guide and everyone was listening. Knowledge is a beautiful thing.

WARNING! WARNING! WARNING!

That informational knife can cut both ways. The Internet now allows everyone to access enlightenment instantly. Anything that comes out of your mouth can be validated immediately. To assume a buyer will not authenticate your input could prove deadly.

Only by having knowledge will you be able to chart a course that keeps you off the reefs, at full sail, in open water. Knowing what is important to your customers allows you to expend effort in those areas that favorably impact them. Trial and error becomes trial and success.

Building successful relationships starts with access to the person you want to sell. Whether they view you as a resource or a waste of time is your call. The tools needed to acquire knowledge are everywhere. Use them! You'll find that as you help your customers overcome their challenges through knowledge, your phone will never stop ringing.

CHAPTER 3

INFLUENCE A
POSITIVE PERCEPTION

Seek only the respect of those you respect.

After reading an article in *Forbes* about getting ahead in business, I decided to enroll at the University of Southern California to earn a master's degree.

What I thought would be an educationally rewarding and productive experience turned out to be one of the most painful periods of my life. No, there weren't any night parachute jumps, no twenty-mile forced marches, and the full equipment, five-mile Ranger runs were a thing of the past. The pain manifested itself as mental anguish. Not because getting a master's degree in systems management is particularly difficult; the suffering comes from knowing that what you are learning has very little utility in the real world. It's painful when you realize that all those hours of discussion and study will probably never be applied, at least not in selling.

The empiricism required to build a bridge is not needed in building a relationship. The universal truths that enable scientists to put satellites in orbit do not apply when urging a customer to put his signature on an order form. It happens only when the customer feels good about his situation and about you as the salesman.

The customer's perceptions about all things great and small trigger actions that either reward or punish your performance.

The only reality that exists takes residence in the customer's mind and it determines where the relationship goes. His reality must become your reality.

If you are going to develop an emotional bond with your customer, there is nothing more important than creating an image that impacts favorably on his consciousness. People act on what they see.

GENESIS 101

At the beginning of any relationship, your initial behavior creates an impression that the customer, at some future date, acts upon. Are your actions in harmony with how she sees things, or are they a cacophonous collection of miscues? Do you project an image of a person with integrity, knowledge, sense of urgency, commitment, and compassion, or do your ill-advised periodic departures from common courtesy paint a picture of you as an unprofessional dolt?

If you are having difficulty in your selling endeavors, there is a good chance you lack a fundamental understanding of the importance of creating positive perceptions.

I can tell you from first-hand experience that many individuals who have ascended to the highest levels in our society are severely lacking in a number of humanistic attributes. They aren't particularly smart, they're selfish, abusive, predisposed to egoism, and in many cases, insecure. On a scale of one to ten, they are a three.

It's difficult these days to pick up a paper and not read about someone we've idolized being knocked off his pedestal. It shocks us to find out that the emotional make-up of the private person is far different from the public person. How did he get so far?

Our idol learned how to influence perceptions. The majority of his overt behavior was characterized by good deeds. He forced himself to do things that his audience liked, and in doing so, established an image that others wanted to support. His shortcomings only occurred behind closed doors.

Now, for every maladjusted miscreant that has made it to the top through deception, there are a hundred that got there legitimately. But I suspect they were no less aggressive in portraying their positive attributes while keeping less desirable tendencies undercover.

It just makes sense. People do not want a relationship with someone whom they view negatively. The more your actions parallel someone else's view of how he thinks things should be, the quicker your emotional bond will come.

SOME FACTS ABOUT IMPRESSIONS:

- *They are created instantly.*
- *First impressions die hard.*
- *Everything you do makes a greater or lesser impression than you think.*
- *Actions impress far more than rhetoric.*

Very few buyers develop strong relationships with salesmen whose behavior runs counter to what they think is correct. The Motivationally Accelerated relationship is one in which the salesman identifies what is important to the buyer and displays behavior that ties to it.

BUYERS:

- *Want to feel they are special.*
- *Expect quick responses*
- *Love creativity.*
- *Admire courage.*
- *Disdain deceit.*
- *Need consistency.*
- *Hate excuses.*

- *Are generally fair.*
- *Give business to salesmen they like.*

MOTIVATIONAL ACCELERATORS:

- *Place their customers on a pedestal.*
- *Are imprisoned by their desire to do what the customer wants.*
- *View no request as too small or too big to be acted upon.*
- *Differentiate themselves from their competition.*
- *Remind their customers how important the relationship is to them.*
- *Are incapable of deceit.*
- *Are considerate, consistent, and credible.*
- *React quickly to every situation*
- *Are consumed by a desire for results.*

I'm well aware that you bought this book because you want to sell better. You are also hoping that much of what you learn will identify activities that make a greater impact while requiring less effort.

Those are my feelings exactly. I have no desire to spend long periods of time accomplishing something. Quick and easy is always better. What matters is results!

As a salesman looking to make an impact there are certain attributes that are required to accelerate situations. Hopefully, they are presently part of your make-up. If not, you should work on acquiring them. But no attribute, regardless of how wonderful, is of any use to you if the customer does not observe it. She will only respond to what she sees. Given that, it's imperative you display as many of your positive characteristics as you can while refraining from showing your warts. Accelerate, don't Decelerate. Motivational Accelerators do things that help them project an image that the customer feels good about. I could give you a hundred examples but I think you're smart enough to grasp the concept with one.

A FERRARI FOR SIXTY-NINE CENTS

Do you want your customers to think you care about them? It's a rhetorical question, of course you do. Is that the perception you create when you do something for them during a business day? Possibly, or maybe not. Buyers aren't stupid! Whatever you do during work hours ties directly to your desire to get something from them. They know it and therefore your actions are more self-centered than customer-directed. No points.

If you're a Motivational Accelerator, your concern is genuine and you want them to know it. It's important they think they're never far from your thoughts. Even during your vacation, a period when you should be relaxing and enjoying your time away, they are with you. So you let them know by sending a postcard or maybe even a small gift to express your feelings. It costs virtually nothing in time and effort, but the impact is substantial. Your thoughtfulness is not viewed as a setup for another order, but rather is interpreted as a thank you for the business. Major score.

Over the years I've observed hundreds of salesmen in action. Many of them worked very hard at being successful. They failed. They never figured out how the game was played. It wasn't what they were that mattered, it got down to what the customer thought they were. They were never able to look at themselves from their customer's point of view. They knew nothing about Motivational Acceleration. They had no idea that stupid actions cost them points. For every Accelerator they employed, they negated it with a Decelerator. They stayed in the Non-Event.

For some unknown reason they thought their customers would embrace mediocrity: Their Accelerators would be rewarded while their Decelerators would be quickly forgiven and forgotten. Using that kind of logic, they will spend their selling career adrift in the doldrums.

Perceptions are easily influenced. If you need a guidance mechanism to keep your efforts on track, I suggest you use the Golden Rule. It's not much more complicated than that.

BRING HIM ANOTHER BEER

Joan Benik understands the concept perfectly. There are lots of restaurants around that serve good food and drink but there are few whose owner makes you feel so overwhelmingly welcome that you start to believe you are a relative. From the moment you walk through her door and she greets you, her warmth and friendliness makes an impression. You're not sure whether she is your mother or sister. It doesn't matter. You're family! Now when decision time rolls around and you are making your choice for a Friday night feast, are you going to go to a stranger's for beers or Aunt Joan's?

The last time I attempted to go elsewhere I felt like Benedict Arnold. The guilt almost killed me. Joan takes a few minutes to make me feel special and in return I give her my wallet. A terrific financial return by anyone's standard.

There are lots of ways to influence positive perceptions.

INTELLIGENCE

Remember what I said about knowledge? Virtually anyone can acquire it. The reality is that of the ten individuals you may be in competition with, at least two are as knowledgeable in key areas as yourself. Your challenge is to break away from the pack by establishing a perception of superior intellect. Let's do a little analysis on the subject of intelligence. Whether your IQ was 165 or 90, if you kept silent, no one would know. There is a lesson to be learned here. Speak and you may be found out. It's been said empty heads have long tongues. If your head is empty, fill it up fast, but until you do, you may find that silence is golden.

An interesting dynamic of silence is that when it exists, people contemplate why it exists. Usually they give you the benefit of the doubt; they assume you must be contemplating the big stuff.

Over the years individuals have been identified to me as geniuses, and as I got to know them I saw that nothing was farther from the truth. They spoke very little because they had nothing to say. They did understand the process of creating an image about superior intellect by keeping their mouths closed. Periodically, when the forum was right, they would drop a "pearl of wisdom," a quote from Shakespeare, pounds of thrust needed to launch a satellite, or the year the cotton gin was invented, and then they would shut up. The perception was created that they were brainy and people want to be around others of equal or superior intelligence.

As an Accelerator, you want to be an intellectual magnet. It's important that you learn as much as you can about as many things as you can that relate to your customer.

Certainly time is a factor, and it will take time to build your foundation of knowledge. In the interim though, there is nothing that prevents you from creating a perception of being knowledgeable. Acquire a variety of intellectual jewels that you can deposit when the time is right. Make sure they are of interest to your customer. Whether it is a quote, a historical reference, or a helpful hint, when you show your buyer there is something between your ears besides silly putty they'll want another date.

SPEED OF ACTION

A few years ago I was giving the keynote speech at a megaconglomerate's international conference. As part of the program they had a satellite uplink that transmitted the speech to all their locations and to a number of important customers around the world. After my comments, a facilitator asked a number of customers what they required to enter into a relationship. One individual from Australia stated that he wanted four things: speed, speed, speed, and speed.

If you haven't figured it out yet, successful people are in a hurry. They don't try to get from one point to another by bus. They are looking to catch a rocket ship. Do we go to the supermarket with the slowest lines? Do we reward the waitress whose inattention extended our meal an extra hour? Of course not. If you want to win points, go fast. If you want to lose points, go slow.

How you operate is your call. If a buyer asks for assistance with something, don't wait. Respond immediately. If you wait, no points are scored. If you excuse yourself and tell him you need to make a phone call to get it accomplished, voila, you've just exhibited, through action, that what is important to him, is important to you. A Positive Impactor will show up on your scorecard.

Speed has always been in vogue. I can't recall any situation where someone got the brass ring for being last. In the Information Age the time allocated to get things done has been compressed. If your speed of action helps a customer clear his desk, why would he want to do business with anyone else? I do not remember one individual whom I've called on who was not impressed by a sense of urgency. Carry with you an attitude that nothing can be done too swiftly, and you've taken a quantum leap forward in securing your selling success.

In today's world anyone can be slowed by administrative overload, even the salesman. Circumstance may not allow you to move as fast as you would like, but that doesn't mean you can't create a perception of speed.

TELL HER STEVE CALLED

Early on in my selling career, circumstance attempted to turn me into a turtle. My counterpart in the western region quit and because the organization had not believed in succession planning, I was given all his accounts. Overnight the demand on my time was doubled. Because my sales territory encompassed seven states, I lived in airports and the pay phone became my best friend.

Invariably, when I checked for messages the number of customers who wanted to talk to me was inversely proportional to the time I had available. A five-minute departure time ensured double digit need.

No good options here. If I called them but didn't have the time to address their issue, I would decelerate. If I didn't return their call quickly, my lack of responsiveness would also decelerate the situation. What's a guy to do? An approach came one day when I received thirty messages fifteen minutes before a five-hour flight. I knew contact influences perception so I did what I could. I called each account and when the receptionist answered, I responded by saying, please leave a message that Steve returned their call and hung up.

In the six months I did double duty I never had anyone complain about me not getting back to them. The buyer's response, when I finally connected, was usually an apology for missing my phone call.

While you might say my approach was a little underhanded, I would submit that when you are in survival mode, the object is to live to play another day. My approach created a perception; when you call Steve, you get a call back . . . fast. Maybe it wasn't the call back they'd always dreamed about but at least they knew Steve was not operating in the twilight zone.

Lots of salesmen are. How do I know that? Because every time I return someone's phone call he or she thanks me. It must mean there are many who don't return phone calls. When you do, you stand out, and a salesman who stands out can become very popular, very fast.

APPEARANCE

The human brain is a remarkable instrument. At its lowest level of cognitive performance, it accomplishes extraordinary things. Unfortunately, very little of its output is ever seen.

The only way anyone will know the composition of your thoughts is when they appear through action. You will be measured by what you say, what you do, and how you look. If that's the case, then cover all your operational bases; act, speak, and look as if your life depended on it. It does! How you are packaged will impact more than access, it will also determine a perception of value.

Successful high-end marketers understand the concept. Take a pound of rice and put it in box and you get a $1.20. Put it in a twenty-five cent hemp bag with a colorful stencil and that same starch gets $3.50.

Package yourself better and you will find buyers are willing to pay a little more to see the guy with the double-breasted baseball cap.

IT WORKED

One good thing about a long commute to work is that you have plenty of time to think. On my five-hour train ride to and from New York I grew tired of thinking through the world's problems. One day I picked up a copy of *Women's Wear Daily* and read about the money to be made in the apparel industry. I decided it was time to become a "Rag Man." I would create a name, design some products, find a manufacturer, and sell a zillion.

The name arrived the next day—Osoli. The company would initially produce the finest sports cap made, so it was imperative I locate a world class manufacturer. The plan seemed simple enough. Six months later the only thing I had to show for my effort was frustration. I quicky found out that skilled manufacturers weren't walking the streets looking for business. They were already working for Ralph, Vera, and Georgio. Convincing them to make products for a company that had no track record of success was as easy as swimming through the La Brea tar pits. Many of my calls went unreturned, and when I did get through, they weren't interested.

Being a novice in the business, I didn't understand how things worked. Then it came to me. At the end of a phone line, I sounded like everyone else. I had no name, no credibility, and no success. How many similar calls did they receive in a week? The strategy materialized quickly. I would adopt an in-your-face selling strategy. I would show up at their offices and let my appearance do a lot of my talking for me.

I needed accelerators. I had a red Porsche. I figured it was worth at least five points. Suit? I had nothing that shouted, "villa in St. Moritz."

I purchased a double-breasted Armani that cost almost as much as the car. Another five. I decided my in-your-face footwear would be reptilian. I didn't care for alligator shoes but they did make a statement. I found a pair at half price, $400. Gotta be worth ten. I figured one more Postitive Impactor and I could make my move. I needed something that would scream "Money! Success! Accomplishment!" I decided the coup de grace to my look would be a $12,000 Rolex President with a plain black onyx face and jubilee band. Beautiful!

Long story short, when I showed up at their doors and let my shoes do the talking, everyone wanted to play. Within months, Osoli was up and running.

Something triggered a change in attitude, and to this day I believe much of it had to do with appearance. At the other end of a phone line, my appearance was anything their mind conjured up. No sale! When I sat in front of them, speculation was removed. The car, the suit, the shoes, and the watch were a reality. I must have been a success. They wanted to grab my coattails and ride me to the promised land. I might be wrong but I'm not going to call Shelly Luna of Atlas Headware to find out. I'd hate to think those alligator shoes I haven't worn since were a waste of money.

GENEROSITY

Santa Always Has a Place at the Table!

The last time you went to dinner with friends and the bill came, did you divide it equally among participants, or did someone at the table convince the group that each person should pay for exactly what they consumed, right down to the peach cobbler?

As you dissected the check and allocated financial responsibility to each party, what thoughts went through your mind? What impression did that person who made the suggestion make on you? generous, successful, accomplished or unsuccessful, cheap, and struggling?

Maybe no such perceptions were created. Friends have a way of overlooking other friends' shortcomings. Friends will, but customers won't. Your customer is the key to your financial success, and I can assure you the customer knows exactly what she has given and what has been received in return. It may not be logged in a journal, but it is indelibly etched in her mind. The customer knows the score!

One of the best ways to show your appreciation for what the customer gives you is through acts of generosity. Giving something back is smart selling for a number of reasons:

- *It shows you understand the give and take of relationships.*
- *You create a perception of success.*
- *It creates a subliminal indebtedness.*

If you haven't figured it out yet, giving to others is an emotionally rewarding way to go through life. My experience is that a majority of the successful people around are givers. Our society is built on people giving to people. I've also come to the conclusion that parsimony is an anathema to a successful relationship. I can turn to Hollywood to support my case.

"It's a Wonderful Life," a timeless Christmas classic about giving, generates tears and cheers, while "Wall Street," a short-lived film about greed, has already been forgotten. Santa Claus is a hero, while Scrooge generates feelings of disdain.

I found out by accident how important it is for others to give to someone who has given something to them. My acts of generosity growing up had no basis in financial gain. For some unknown reason, I was given a Santa Claus gene. I couldn't control myself from giving what I had to others. The interesting thing was that as I gave, I received. At the time, I didn't understand the human dynamic that governs such action, I just accepted it.

If you are a Motivational Accelerator, I have to believe you want the most from life. Understand this! The more you give to your customers, the more they will give back. There will be periodic exceptions, and when you encounter them, adjust. In those professional and personal relationships that are worth accelerating, generosity will be rewarded. The corn will pop.

RALPH HERRMANNS

A number of winters ago, I was looking to escape the cold and decided to tour the Caribbean with the final leg of my trip culminating in Haiti. I had checked into the Hotel Olafson in Port Au Prince, and as I walked to my room, a gentleman passed by me who appeared to be in pain. I had some aspirin with codeine left over from a back injury, so when I saw him at the pool, I offered it. He accepted, and in gratitude extended a dinner invitation.

It turned out the gentleman happened to be Ralph Herrmanns, one of Sweden's literary elite, and a world-renowned figure. His trip to Haiti centered around doing a television documentary. In short, he was so moved by the generosity of a stranger that he invited me to tour the country in a limousine that the Haitian government had provided. The four days I spent with Ralph started an association that has lasted to this day. A small act of kindness for someone I didn't know opened a world to me that I had only read about in books. His residence and associations in Sweden are now at my disposal.

As a humorous gesture, he has found a way to insert the name Steve Sullivan in twenty of his literary works. Periodically, they are hand-delivered to me in New York by one of a number of Swedish luminaries, including industrialists, prominent sculptors, artists, and politicians.

Friends of mine have been entertained by Ralph in Stockholm and used his connections in Sweden to develop their business relationships. It is a lifetime friendship that started with $4 worth of medication.

SAM AND VICKI SEBASTIANI

In the world of wine, Sam and Vicki Sebastiani are recognized as two of the wine industry's most dynamic people. On a flight to Europe I read an article about their departure from the family wine business and how they were in the process of starting their own winery, Viansa.

The article so impressed me that I sent them both a few Osoli products with a note that said, "Good luck!" They responded quickly with an invitation to visit their winery!

In the interim, I continued to read about the incredible environment they were creating at Viansa. I sent them a congratulatory note and a few Osoli t-shirts. They sent back a case of wine.

Three weeks later Osoli showed up on *Lifestyles of the Rich and Famous* when Jon Sebastiani wore a t-shirt during the Viansa segment. I visited the winery shortly thereafter and received a royal tour. That treatment is also given to my network of friends and business associates when they visit wine country.

Over the years our families have vacationed together and the friendship is growing. My wine cabinet is filled with some of the finest wine in the world, Viansa, and I paid nothing for it. Can I put a price on the friendship? No, but I do know the start-up cost was $32.50.

BRUCE KILLEN

If you don't own a work of art by Bruce Killen, I can understand why. As one of the world's top bronze sculptors, Bruce's masterpieces are very expensive.

While on a Rogue River rafting trip, I had to fly out of the Medford, Oregon, airport. As I waited, I noticed a showcase filled with magnificent wildlife sculptures. A promotional piece stated Bruce lived in the area.

I had three hours to kill so I checked the phone book for his number. I wanted to call and tell him how much I admired his work. He answered and said he lived on a mountain top just minutes from the airport. An invitation was extended to visit his studio. I grabbed a taxi and a short time later I stood at his front door. The following two hours were as educationally rewarding as any I have spent. I learned about sculpting and Bruce Killen.

I also found out Bruce knew something about selling. As any Motivational Accelerator knows, give and you shall receive. On the flight back to New York I thought about what Bruce had done for me and wanted to reciprocate. I bought two bronzes. Three months later Bruce sent me a complimentary bronze quail. I reciprocated by purchasing a bear. This went on for a few years. He gave, I bought. He gave, I bought. On the verge of bankruptcy I called Bruce Killen and pleaded with him not to send me any more free bronzes. His reply was, "Not a chance Steve, Santa always has a place at the table." Embrace that concept and over time you'll find that generosity will create opportunities you didn't know existed.

Motivational Accelerators understand the dynamics of giving perfectly. They also know how to give to make the greatest impact.

- *They give unconditionally.*
- *They time the delivery of the gift.*
- *They downplay its worth.*
- *They separate themselves from the act of giving and a desire to receive.*

Note: It's not what you give that's important, the thought behind the action is where the Acceleration lies.

Non-Accelerators do just the opposite.

▪ *They create an impression that there are strings attached.*

▪ *They give shortly before they want to receive.*

▪ *They emphasize the value of the gift, not realizing the receiver will determine its worth.*

▪ *What they give is a small fraction of what they are capable of giving.*

A Non-Accelerator thinks that generosity squanders resources. A Motivational Accelerator understands that giving can get the receiving started. Just ask the Japanese. Their society is built around the act of gift-giving. Try building a relationship with a Japanese executive without giving gifts. Instead of a limousine picking you up at the airport, you'll find yourself hitchhiking. If you choose not to be generous for the added dimension it gives to your life, do it for survival!

BEWARE—A GENEROUS COMPETITOR WILL EAT YOU ALIVE!!

When you are down to your last nickel, don't spend it. Give it away and it will probably return as a quarter.

YOU'RE KIDDING

Five years ago I caught the antique bug. I think my wife would have preferred anthrax. Few weekends pass where I'm not in pursuit of a treasure. Last year, I stumbled into the Saltbox antique shop on Barnum Square in Bethel, Connecticut. A magnificently framed photo caught my eye. Upon closer scrutiny, I saw that the picture was that of American icon P.T. Barnum. The gold scroll lettering at the bottom of the picture indicated the photo had been taken by renowned photographer Elmer Clickering. Incredibly, at the base of the photo was

Barnum's waxed seal and a personal handwritten note to Frank Sherwood Esq.

Having seen an autographed Annie Oakley postcard auctioned for $11,000 my heart jumped out of my chest. It had to be worth six figures. "How much is the photo?" I inquired. "It's not for sale," came his response. "The Barnum Museum has been trying to buy it for years," he added. "I can see why," I replied, as I fell into disconsolate depression.

Over a period of six months I frequently visited the shop. I liked the owner, so when I found out he was erudite, I would always bring in something of intellectual interest. I did so with no underlying motive.

On one sweltering July day, I brought him a large lemonade. His enthusiastic thank you was surprising. You would have thought I'd given him tickets to the moon. As he fell into silence, I could see he was contemplating something major. A question broke the tranquility. "You like that Barnum picture don't you?" he asked. It was a rhetorical question. "Give me two hundred dollars and it's yours," he stated.

The moment he made the offer he forfeited a big payday. Or maybe he got a big payday. In the course of human events it is not uncommon for one act of generosity to be countered by another. Have you ever been generous to someone else? Give it a try, you may like the feeling. Are people impacted by generosity? Yes, and other things too.

ASSOCIATIONS

I was asked recently to identify my greatest selling asset, and without a moment's hesitation I replied, "exposure." When you've lived in twenty-nine places in fifty years, you've had countless associations; with people, places, and things. It's been a long time since I've been with someone whom I didn't share something in common with.

We want our customers to feel good about us. If we delivered a monologue about the essence of our goodness, it would be long-winded, self-serving, and tiresome. You don't need to. Let your associations do the talking. It is a far quicker way to influence a customer's perception of you.

Each association, in whatever form it takes, carries with it a history and reputation. In most associations, your connection came about by choice and therefore, whatever image it carries will, in some way, be projected onto you. Right or wrong, it happens.

Your customers have associations also. When their interests coincide with yours, Acceleration takes place. Deceleration occurs when your associations come into conflict.

I GOT MY KICKS ON ROUTE 66

In retrospect it served as a great learning experience, although at the time I viewed it as anything but educational. In the late seventies, I had just been given my DD Form 214, indicating that my resignation from the army had been accepted and that "soldier" no longer described my occupation. Corporate America awaited me in San Francisco and I had five days to get there.

My BMW 3.0CS could cruise at 130 m.p.h., so maybe I would do the trip in a day and a half. Whatever the time frame, I knew I would exceed the speed limit, so I strategically hung my class A army uniform in the back window. I'd discovered a few years earlier state troopers had a sympathetic soft spot for army officers. I think it has something to do with protecting the country or a shared value system on guns, Mom, and apple pie. Whatever their thinking, it engenders an attitude of "give the speeder a break" and with a 2,800-mile journey ahead of me, I thought I might need a few breaks.

In looking at the map, I decided to take historic Route 66 across the country. As I blew through city after city, I began to realize that the TV series had overstated the adventure to be found along the roadway. I would be in Oklahoma City in an hour and hadn't had a thrill yet. After fourteen hours of driving, weariness had set in, and I decided to look for a motel. By the time I found one, my watch said

0100 hours and they were closed for the night. I had a sleeping bag in the trunk so I really didn't care. I would find a rest area near the highway and save twenty dollars. I got off at the next exit and proceeded optimistically down a country back road. I knew the perfect spot would be found right around the bend.

Thirty miles up the road, my optimism gone, I decided the location no longer had to be perfect. It only had to accommodate the length and width of my car. Within seconds of having changed the criteria for my sleeping accommodations, a dirt road appeared to the left. It looked inviting. As I pulled in my lights illuminated a fence and an open gate. A sign on the fence post said, not surprisingly, "No Trespassing."

It runs counter to my value system to violate someone's right to privacy, so initially, I had no intention of entering the field beyond the fence, but lack of sleep facilitates delinquent behavior.

The clock on the dashboard now read 0200 hours and I started to rationalize that no trespassing only applied to people who were planning on homesteading. I would only be there a couple of hours. Hell, I'd spend the past six years protecting their lifestyle. I had an entitlement.

I would pull in just far enough so I wasn't visible from the road. Within moments of entering the property, I detected something wasn't right. The night radiated a cold, damp blackness . . . and my tires were spinning in the mud. I immediately turned off the engine and got out of my car to see what had transpired. I pulled out a flashlight, and as I turned it on, a sickening feeling overcame me. The two rear tires had just dug the Erie Canal in some farmer's cornfield. My German friend and I were stuck!

After going through the alphabet of epithets, I decided I would confront my predicament in the morning. I pulled out my sleeping bag and crawled in.

I guess I fell asleep immediately, because I don't remember anything until excruciating pain brought me to consciousness. My ribs felt like they had exploded. This is a dream, I thought. The next blow to my buttocks assured me it wasn't.

Four letter words seemed to be coming from all directions. Dazed, I climbed out of my bag and stood up. The light shone in my eyes blinded me and an object was immediately pressed against my cheek. "Move and I'll blow your f . . . ng head off." Over the next few minutes, they called me a variety of derogatory names. Both gentlemen were working themselves into a frenzy. I probably would have been more frightened had I not been in so much pain.

I told them I hadn't seen the "No Trespassing" sign. At that point the individual with the gun against my face stated, "We shoot trespassers around here." I hoped he said that for effect.

As I stood in my underpants, wondering where the situation was headed, the second gentlemen searched my car. Immediately, he saw my uniform hanging in the back window. "Are you in the army?" he inquired. I quickly evaluated my choices for a response and lied, "Yes, I'm on my way to Fort Sill." Immediately something caught his interest. "Are you airborne?" he asked. He knew the answer the moment he saw the parachutist badge on my uniform. "Yes," I said. "I was airborne," he stated. "I spent two years in the 82nd."

Immediately silence blanketed us. You could feel him processing my input. "I'll be back when it's light to pull you out," he said.

As quickly as it began, the encounter ended. They were gone within moments. At daybreak, he showed up and pulled my car out. Virtually no words were exchanged. No apology was given.

I suspect he didn't like me much more than the night before, but because we were members of the same club "paratrooper," he felt an obligation to assist me. Periodically, I reflect back on the experience and wonder what would have happened had I put my uniform in the trunk.

Associations are a great catalyst to get Acceleration started. Everyone is looking for common ground. It helps with the communication process. It allows you to interface in an area where you both have knowledge. The concept is pretty simple to understand: A friend of a friend is a friend. But it can also lead to Deceleration; associating with enemies creates enemies.

INSIDER OR OUTSIDER

As you evaluate your own inventory of associations, recognize that you don't have to be a fellow member of Greenpeace to cement a relationship. In most instances, a change in perception will start to occur the moment another individual realizes you have something in common.

I once showed up at a business meeting in West Texas dressed like a Wall Street banker and when I sat down at the table on a scorching July afternoon, the temperature at the table was frigid. I was an outsider and I'm sure they thought I looked like a charter member of the "quiche club."

Over time I got a little smarter. I realized that the environment was rough and tough. Clint, red meat, and Harley Davidson were king. No sissies allowed. If I was going to make it I'd better adapt. Art, classical music, and tennis were associational playing cards that would not be dealt.

Sunday morning rides on my Harley, pumping iron at the gym, or pulling the trigger on a Canadian goose, now that's what life is all about. It never failed. In a short period of time, I'd go from foreigner to friend.

I've known salesmen who had no success at selling a buyer, no matter how hard they worked, until it became evident they shared a meaningful association. That association was the ignition spark that got the relationship moving.

In order to get going in the right direction, I recommend that you do a little investigative research. Find out about your customer's interests, likes, and dislikes. Never forget that the tendency of many people is to look for the worst in people instead of the best. Don't give your buyer an excuse not to do business with you.

WORTH MORE THAN YOU THOUGHT

There are many challenges when you work in New York City, none bigger than finding a great new deli where you can buy your lunch.

It normally happens in one of two ways: a coworker makes a suggestion, or you walk the streets until some gastronomic indicator tells you this is "the place."

Actually, there was a time when there were three ways. The third was you would call Robert DeNiro and ask him. You see, DeNiro has eaten in every deli in New York. At least, I think he has. Why else would his picture be in all their windows? It has even appeared in a pet food store. Did Bobbie actually eat there or was it his rotweiler?

It does get confusing. What about that window that showcased Andre, Bobbie, and Brooke. Were they all there together? How did she like her Reuben? It must have been great or she wouldn't have given them her picture. Or did she?

It wasn't until one October afternoon when I stepped in to grab a bite at Otto's Dim Sum that I started to suspect that framed photos on the wall didn't necessarily mean an endorsement. When I received my Moo Goo Gai Pan and it tasted like dog food, I figured it out.

Frank Sinatra's words came crashing down, "If you can make it there, you can make it anywhere." How true. The competition is fierce. To survive in the Big Apple, you have to use every available resource. Why not Lassie?

Is it deceptive? I think not. It's called promotion. If you are going to Accelerate, you had better learn how to promote yourself. If you can't, you'll spend your life running with the pack.

It's understood that individuals want to associate with successful people. That's why most of life's washouts are not only broke but lonely. Call it the "coattail principle." If you create a perception of success, others will want to hang on for the ride. They will try to use you, and in return you will find ways to use them. There is nothing wrong with that. People using people is how the world evolved.

Putting a celebrity photo in your window is the pictorial equivalent of being a name dropper. As with anything, you should manage the process. Moderation works best. Dropping one or two names in the course of an evening with your customer is smart selling. You'll score points. Overkilling the technique will get you labeled as a bore. You'll Decelerate quickly.

Most people have a tendency to make great assumptions with very little information. When you provide the perfect "jewel" at the right time, their brains will take off on an intellectual marathon, and when it's finished, you may have conquered the world or at least their part of it.

DO YOU KNOW TOMMY FERRENTINO?

In my business career, I have encountered few individuals as talented as Kim Rendelman. Her resume is a head hunter's dream, and in the twenty years I've known Kim, I've watched her rise to the highest levels of corporate America. As a mover and shaker at Lippencott and Margulies, the corporate image consultants, she was always accepted and included in whatever arena she was operating in, with one exception, Kelsey's Gym.

You see at Kelsey's, the in-crowd is part of the "ceps" gang. If you didn't have bulging biceps, triceps, and quadriceps, you were in the out-crowd. I've been lifting weights since I was twelve so I could appreciate her predicament. Anyone who has ever taken weight training seriously understands that being an outcast makes the gym experience far less rewarding. When that lactic acid enters your muscles after thirty repetitions, and your arms are burning, you need a muscle-head calling you a wimp to spur you on. Kim had none.

She had gotten the weight-lifting bug a few years earlier and for some reason wanted her physical prowess to match her mental acuity. Brains and brawn, what a deadly combination. Sadly enough, she did not inherit the "muscle gene." After a couple months of working out on her own, she realized she would never achieve what she wanted in strength conditioning unless she could work out with the "big boys." The situation appeared hopeless because the only criterion they used was physical appearance. Muscle mass meant everything and Kim had little. What she did possess was an understanding of the power of association.

She knew about my friendship with Tommy Ferrentino, one of the world's top body builders. She asked me if I could get Tommy to sign one of his body shots. He did. It read, "Kim, you are my motivation. Tommy." Somehow that photo found its way to the gym and the ceps gang. They had no idea Kim knew Tommy. If Kim knew Tommy she must be something special. How could she possibly be Tommy Ferrentino's motivation? Obviously, there was more to her than met the eye. Did she also know Cory, Lee, and Arnold? Would she bring them to the gym? It's not surprising that Kim is now a member of the in-crowd. No, I don't know what will happen when Arnold never shows up.

THAT SUITCASE ISN'T MINE

Yes, it is! I've said that when you enter into a relationship you start with a Non-Event. Well, not exactly. Your initial encounter with a buyer may be a Non-Event because you just met, but in the course of an association with your company and all its ancillary entities, there is "a history." As the salesman on the account, you are responsible for the sum of everything the customer feels about the relationship. It comes with the job description. Good, bad, or indifferent, his feelings belong to you.

You thought you started on a level playing field. Life's tough! Previous sales representation, quality problems, and lack of responsiveness have you sliding through the visitor's end zone. The word is out. Your organization and anyone associated with it is a leper. You just got there and you're down 900 points. Implosion isn't far away.

If you want to make an impact, there's no time like the present. Excess baggage is a killer! On the upside, I've found customers to be quite forgiving (the sins of the father shall not be visited on the son), but only if an immediate program of change is implemented. Action, not rhetoric, is essential! First impressions are critical so everything needs to be quickened. Overkill in the first six month's is necessary. It will cement in the customer's mind that you are different. An overabundance of attention, follow-up, and sense of urgency will help counter a legacy of abuse.

A SILVER BULLET

Anyone who has been been involved in selling can recite a litany of war stories where things didn't go according to Hoyle. They were making all the right moves and for some reason their best laid plan was met with rejection.

Because perception is in the eye of the beholder anything you do could be misinterpreted. You thought you were being generous, the buyer thought it was a bribe. Your invitation to conduct training was perceived as arrogance. A Non-Accelerator would use the possibility of action being misperceived as an excuse to do nothing. A Motivational Accelerator sees objections as an opportunity to inject additional clarity into the situation.

Warning: Objections are often delivered in sheep's clothing: "This isn't exactly what we are looking for. I thought your price would be more competitive. Our customer isn't sure your delivery meets their needs." The underlying message is: "I don't like your product. I don't like your price. I don't like your service."

Those feelings may stem more from a perception of your product, price, or service than the reality of your offering. Recognize that buyers are so innundated with information that it's difficult to keep it all straight. If the relationship is going to move forward, you need to identify the real issue and resolve it quickly. You have to become the clarifying agent. Having an objection-handling model to govern your actions will insure a more simplistic and effective approach in countering any obstacles.

AIR IT OUT

One of the most difficult activities for an unskilled salesman is overcoming objections. Instead of seeing the objection as an opportunity to resolve doubt, clarify issues, and cement a commitment, Non-Accelerators see objections as a personal attack and threat to their success. They become defensive, initiate a counter attack, and in most instances fail to address the issue at hand. What they don't rec-

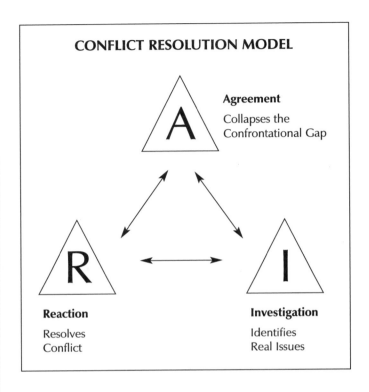

CONFLICT RESOLUTION MODEL

A

Agreement

Collapses the
Confrontational Gap

R

I

Reaction

Resolves
Conflict

Investigation

Identifies
Real Issues

ognize is that an objection, properly handled, will expedite the process of getting the buyer to say yes. In order for any objection to be overcome effectively, a simple model, A-I-R, should be used. It consists of three elements: agreement, investigation, and reaction.

STEP 1: AGREEMENT

When someone objects to something it could be for a variety of reasons. In order to successfully resolve the issue, the salesman should initially agree with the person doing the objecting. The agreement is phrased in a way that lends support to the objector without confirming his claim. If the objector states that "your price is too high," the salesman responds by saying, "I agree that price is an important issue." By delivering a sympathetic response you can support the view of the objector without validating his belief.

Impact: By agreeing with the buyer you have just collapsed the confrontational gap and created some common ground (you both agree price is important). The buyer made a statement and you supported his right to make it. Had you disagreed with the statement, responding that " nobody has ever had a problem with our price," you would have widened the confrontational gap. It is much more difficult to resolve an issue with an enemy than with a friend. When you agree with someone, he will see you as a supporter and be more inclined to allow you to pursue the issue.

STEP 2: INVESTIGATION

In order to resolve any objection it is imperative that you accurately identify a buyer's reality. When a buyer states that "your price is too high," is he talking about affordability or value? Investigating the buyer's input will help uncover what the real facts are. Facts, not speculation, will dictate your response. Formulating investigative questions is simple. They normally begin with who, what, when, where, why, and how.

Impact: By investigating what the buyer says you are showing interest and sensitivity. You can't help but score. You are also accumulating facts that will help determine your course of action.

STEP 3: REACTION

You react because selling is about resolving issues. In any objection-handling situation the issue is not resolved until the buyer confirms that what you are giving him is acceptable.

Impact: You Accelerate the buyer by effectively resolving the problem. Too often salesman perceive that an issue has been resolved when it hasn't. If you get the buyer to agree that the issue no longer exists, there should be no hesitation on the buyer's part to moving forward. Reluctance may indicate that there is another issue unresolved and your use of AIR will be needed again.

LEMONADE: A CASE STUDY

SCENARIO 1

You have just set up a stand in the Mojave Desert selling lemonade for a quarter. A prospective buyer appears on the horizon. As he approaches, you prepare for the encounter. He walks up to your stand tired, dusty, and thirsty, surveys your offering, and states, "Your price is too high." You fear you will lose the sale so you cut your price in half and pour. You pocket a nickel in profit.

SCENARIO 2

You have just set up a stand in the Mojave Desert selling lemonade for a quarter. A prospective buyer appears on the horizon. As he approaches, you prepare for the encounter. He walks up to your stand tired, dusty, and thirsty, surveys your offering, and states, "Your price is too high." As an expert in the use of AIR, you agree that the price is an important issue but do nothing else until you investigate what the individual means by "too high."An investigative question follows, "How much money do you have?" The individual states $1.00. Given the response, you determine it is not an affordability issue.

Another investigative question follows. "Why do you say my price is too high?" His response is direct. The glass is too small, it's dirty, there is no place to sit. Obviously you have a value buyer. Another investigative question follows. "How much do you think you should get for a quarter?" "Six ounces," he replies. You calculate that you can accommodate the request and still make a fifteen-cent profit. The decision comes easily.

Let's extricate you from the beverage business and instead of selling the product for a quarter you are selling systems for a quarter of a million dollars. In the presence of a disgruntled buyer it is easy to make accommodations that are in no one's best interest. I've never met a buyer who wanted a good supplier to go out of business. If you can show a buyer the error of his ways, more often than not he will adjust.

Be advised, the more sizeable the investment, the more likelihood you will encounter resistance. When you find yourself under the kind of pressure that a hostile buyer can engender, having a model to guide your actions will prove useful. With practice, using AIR will become almost as easy as breathing. The next time you get attacked don't give away the store, AIR it out.

CHAPTER 4

BECOME A PRACTICING PSYCHOLOGIST

I've always found it is easier to ride a camel in the direction it's going.

Appearances are deceiving. Just ask Victor Hugo. The Hunchback of Notre Dame was a wonderful guy. He would have been the life of any Parisian cocktail party, but he never received an invitation. It's not surprising, because until you know differently, you act on what you see.

My experience in dealing with others has educated me to the fact that people are dramatically different than the image they project. Some of the the smartest people I know look like Bozo and the toughest human being I've ever known could have been a librarian (no insult intended).

With age and experience, I've gotten much better at not jumping to conclusions about someone until I've observed their behavior over a period of time. I've been surprised so often that I've come to the realization that there is a cosmic law that governs the creation of first impressions . . . they're never correct.

I'll use myself as an example. I believe there is no one who puts a higher price on friendship than me. I hold friendship in such high esteem that there is little I wouldn't do for a friend. Because of this, I can only accommodate so many. Before I bring someone into my inner sanctum, I want to make sure they are worthy of the consideration they will receive.

When I first meet someone, I am cordial but reserved. I probably come across as distant, but I'm not. I just believe that friendships are developed through experience. When your actions indicate to me you understand the give and take of a friendship, I'll be happy to be your friend.

I would hope your customers operate the same way. They save their business for the salesman that is willing to put effort where rhetoric resides. Don't ever forget, you are in competition with lots of others who want the same things as you. Why would a buyer embrace you until you've been tested? In my journey through life, I've found the easier something comes my way, the less value there is in it.

A problem many salesmen encounter is a tendency to judge someone quickly and then act on their initial feelings. I suggest you indulge in a little analysis Don't lump your buyers into one collective bag and sell to them all the same way. If you do, you will connect with a few but miss with the rest. I can guarantee you that the guy wearing the business suit and bow tie has a different psychological make-up than the gentleman with the black t-shirt and cowboy boots. People are unique. Your job as a Motivational Accelerator is to identify the target and select the right ammunition.

In order to do that you need to become a practicing psychologist. Ignore what comes out of someone's mouth, it's probably part of his act, his facade. Watch his actions; they are the key to what makes him tick. Don't focus on the big stuff. Everyone talks about trust, respect, and forgiveness. Anyone can preach the gospel, only people with integrity live it. I don't know about you but I find that when I'm involved with a buyer who understands fairness, I not only benefit financially but also emotionally.

Little things will pinpoint whether a buyer understands the give and take of a relationship. Does your customer keep you waiting? Does he thank you for your effort? Does he reciprocate with acts of thoughtfulness?

Answering no to all those questions doesn't mean you terminate the relationship; it will allow you to prioritize where you expend the greatest effort. Giving to someone who never gives back is no way to stay energized. When you think someone is worthy, go for the gusto.

BORN IN BIRMINGHAM

A few years back I was called by my regional sales manager and told we had a monumental problem in the South. The first order for a potentially huge customer had arrived with quality problems. They wanted to return it and as far as they were concerned our new relationship was over.

I immediately called the president, who had a reputation as uncompromising and tough, and requested a meeting. He told me his schedule was full but he would rearrange it. Hmm. An uncompromising, stubborn lout showing flexibility. "What's going on here?" I thought.

When was good for me, he asked. Another surprise. Consideration! We set a time and the next day I arrived in Birmingham. Surprisingly, his driver was at the airport to pick us up. Holy cow. Thoughtful. The meeting lasted three hours and in the course of the discussion we determined our mistake would cost them but they would work through it. Another surprise. Understanding! His invitation to treat us to the best meal in town was the culmination of a serendipitous experience.

Once again I'd been taught reputation means nothing. Ignore what you hear, act on what you see, and more often than not you can create your own existence. To this day I've never had a better business relationship

Psychologists have attempted to explain behavior in a variety of ways, with numbers, letters, and adjectives. Some of it makes sense. Much of it doesn't. Remember what we said about marketing. Clever sells, but it doesn't necessarily help you accelerate relationships.

In my simple way of relating to different buyer types I've created what I call a Compatibility Index. I want to expend my time and effort with buyers whose psychological make-up is compatible with mine. Spending one's life as a combatant is no way to perpetuate a career.

The Compatability Index consists of three areas: generosity, security, and initiative. While people possess myriad idiosyncratic behaviors, I've found that when these three traits are present the probability for a successful partnership is greater.

Generosity: Selling involves give and take. There should be no one-way streets. As you give to your customer he is supposed to give something back. Your time and energy needs to be rewarded. Some buyers understand it, others don't. I'm constantly evaluating what a buyer has done for me. Over time if I determine nothing, I may take my time and resources and put them elsewhere.

It should come as no surprise that the world is full of of takers. The term is not meant to carry any negative connotation. I know a lot of wonderful people who are predominantly takers. They give, but their psychological orientation finds more pleasure in receiving. They do require a different selling strategy. Tactics need to be developed.

A taker will develop a relationship only if he perceives he will receive something tangible from it. He gives in order to receive. If accommodating you gets more for him, you will be accommodated. The carrot and stick approach works very well with takers. Motivationally Accelerated relationships gravitate toward balance. Our credo: when you take . . . give. When you give . . . take.

Security: Security is all about confidence. How confident is your buyer? When you are around him do you have to walk on eggshells? Is every comment scrutinized? People who lack confidence tend to hesitate. They gravitate to the status quo because they see protection there. An insecure buyer will eat up a lot of your time. In some cases it's worth it, in others it isn't.

Initiative: When you find a buyer with initiative you have struck gold. Moving ahead in all relationships requires a willingness to act. As necessary as action is to the process, it is a commodity in short supply. Isaac Newton understood the concept and described it in his first law of motion. "A body at rest will remain at rest unless it encounters an external force." Your accelerating behaviors can provide the external force but recognize that the initiative of the buyer will determine your impact.

Earlier, when discussing the Spectrum of Influence, we stated that we need to quantify behavior so we can measure it. The same holds with the Compatibility Index.

Once again the numbers are small. I score buyers between one and five in the areas of generosity, security, and initiative. If their cumulative total doesn't hit at least ten they come off the A-list. I may still call on them but I save the best stuff for buyers who are compatible.

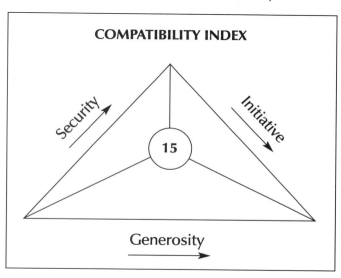

SINCE ADAM AND EVE

Attempting to explain what makes people act has occupied the thoughts of intellectuals if not since Adam and Eve at least since Socrates. What makes one individual pick up a sword and another individual put it down? Some believe a predisposition for action is learned, while others think it is genetic. For our purposes, let's eschew analysis in favor of identification. From my own experience, I've come to the conclusion that there are four distinct buyer types with regard to a willingness to act: Informationalist, Machinist, Constructionist, and Opportunist.

Informationalist: A buyer whose modus operandi is chararacterized by a penchant for facts. No matter how simple the issue, he wants more facts. Facts, facts, and more facts. The buyer will not act unless he has enough facts and he can never seem to get enough facts. All issues are prolonged ad infinitum. When engaging an Informationalist a salesman puts success on hold. The question becomes is the pay-day worth the wait. In most cases I would say no.

Machinist: A buyer who wants hands on involvement with all aspects of the relationship. If she doesn't get to touch, see, and smell everything she doesn't want to participate. Buy her a uniform, invite her into the dugout, and let her drink from the water fountain. If she gets to play she will be happy to pay.

Constructionist: A buyer that will not act unless he feels that systems are in place to support whatever actions are taken. His holistic approach to operational integrity insures that nothing falls through the cracks. Constructionists make suppliers better. In order to meet their demands, you will have to cover all the bases. Do not try to sell a Constructionist on a wing and a prayer. When price, quality, service, and delivery are integreted into one complete package and supported with ancillary programs, the deal is yours. They'll get on board.

Opportunist: A buyer that is addicted to action. You gotta love it, but beware. This MO has its pros and cons. An Opportunist can't wait to get going but in many instances hasn't had time to think through the ramifications of the action. The buyer's Ready, Fire, Aim approach often gets supplier and seller in trouble.

CHAPTER 5

PERSONALIZE THE RELATIONSHIP

Be liked and you will never want.

In the course of getting to this stage in my life, I've been involved in a number of high-risk ventures. I've jumped out of airplanes at midnight, rappelled from helicopters, kayaked through class eight rapids, dived off cliffs, and started a number of companies.

Each adventure, in its own way terrified me, but nothing generated more fear than starting a business relationship with Randy Stapleford.

James Bond? No, Randy Stapleford. A lot of people confuse the two. The adjectives are similar: debonair, worldly, precise, professional, caring, knowledgeable, and lethal. That's right, lethal; James in the business of espionage, and Randy in the business of getting people to give him what he wants.

My relationship with Captain Stapleford started as a footnote when I met him at the Viansa Winery. As the Director of the Naval Staff College he was accompanying a class of international naval officers on a tour of the country. The elite group was receiving an education on democracy by getting to witness the best America had to offer. I was in the area so they asked if I would give a brief talk on leadership.

When Sam Sebastiani introduced Randy Stapleford to me he concluded the introduction by saying, "Watch this guy, he'll pick your pocket." I was intrigued by the comment so I queried Stapleford as to what Sebastiani meant by it. "I have no idea," he replied. I turned to Sebastiani for an explanation. "How does a navy guy pick your pocket?" I asked.

"Easily," he responded. "The Captain brings forty sailors to the winery to eat, drink, and make merriment and I subsidize the event." "You're a nice guy," I commented. "I can't help myself," he responded.

Little did I know my pocket was about to be picked. When I returned home I found a letter waiting from Captain Stapleford. With it was an autographed picture of the international class, a War College cap, and key chain. In addition, an invitation was extended for my wife and I to visit Newport and stay with the Stapleford family. "Nice guy," I thought.

Two weeks later a formal invitation was extended to address the new incoming class. Unfortunately, as he pointed out, there was no honorarium available to pay for it. I agreed to participate. Shortly thereafter, a package arrived with some additional items for my wife and kids and another request. Would it be possible to bring a few leadership books that the class could pass around. He stated he would love to buy the books but the budget didn't allow for it. I responded with complimentary books for everyone.

Additional requests have come my way with the my response always being the same, I'll be happy to oblige. I can't imagine turning him down. I take solace in knowing there are myriad others who have fallen prey to his magic. Actually there is no magic in it. He's a wonderful guy and he doesn't hide it from you. His approach embodies the essence of Motivational Acceleration.

His formula for success is simple. He establishes contact, makes you feel warm and fuzzy, focuses his attention on your family, hobbies, and interests, then makes a request. You give it gladly because his transition from friend to salesman is so smooth, you would tell your mother "no" before Stapleford.

The logic behind his actions is not revolutionary. He knows, as do all Motivational Accelerators, that making your "target of opportunity" your friend is smart business. The target becomes more willing, open, loyal, honest, and consistent than when he or she was a stranger. It requires time and effort outside the normal nine-to-five business day.

Why is it critical to be involved with someone after business hours? Remember the discussion on perception? Customers are not stupid. They perceive, when you interact with them while they're working, that your actions are self-centered. Your performance has one objective—an order.

When you focus on non-job-related activities, you send a different message. The customer now is not sure of the motivation behind what you are doing.

Are your expressions of kindness, thoughtfulness, generosity, and concern a product of financial greed, or is it because you care about him or her as a human being? Your behavior, not your rhetoric, will make the statement for you. Individuals will always find a way to do business with someone they like.

Friendship transcends many boundaries. If your customer is your friend, everything that is important to him is of concern to you. What have you done to reflect your attitude? Did you send him a get-well card when he was sick? A birthday wish? A postcard when you were on vacation? Did you help a friend of his get an interview? Did you save that article on Little League baseball for his son? Have you had him to your home? Did you buy that silver spoon in England for his wife's collection? When was the last time you brought his cherished Golden Retriever something? When he told you he was going to the Caribbean on vacation, did you get him some sunscreen? Were you as readily available during his last crisis as you were when his last order was up for grabs?

As you can see, there is nothing particularly profound or complex in developing strong, long-lasting business relationships. Much of it is a matter of focus. Is yours inward or outward?

Who is more important, you or your customer? Like any successful marriage, if the partnership is a friendship, both parties are giving far more than they are taking. When the columns of activity are totaled, and the bottom line is determined, each individual made out just fine.

This past year I've spent time with Randy Stapleford and have gotten to observe his selling style up close and personal; with me and with others, the fundamentals never vary.

We don't need forty adjectives to describe his actions when one will do. Randy Stapleford, like any great Motivational Accelerator, makes the people he associates with feel special. They feel cared about and respected. They believe their best interests are in the forefront of his thoughts. They know he likes them because he expresses it in hundreds of different ways. They are rewarded in some way for what they give to the relationship.

Does Randy put a lot of time and effort into building relationships? Yes! But he would tell you that there is no better place to spend his life than with friends. He does so knowing that the pay back will be tenfold. I am not sure when the next phone call will come. I know it will; I'm just hoping he won't ask for my firstborn. I'd have to say yes.

Do I know that often, even though we are friends, I am being sold, and I will be expected to give something up? Of course I do! But so what? In living life, I am always going to have to give something to somebody; so why not give it to someone I like and respect? Let the jerks go hungry!

WHEN SMOKE GETS IN YOUR EYES

A principle component of Motivational Acceleration is speed. Getting to the heart of issues is imperative if you are going to close sales rapidly. Identifying what penetrates the "Threshold of Significance" is critical. In every relationship, a sea of extra-

neous nonsense surrounds what is important to you and your customer. Cutting through it is a must. I've found through experience that there aren't ten issues that will determine sales success; usually it's no more than two.

As with throwing darts, you get the big score when you hit the bull's-eye. Being able to see the bull's-eye helps. When you personalize relationships, your customer will be more open and honest. She, in fact, may be incapable of giving you an order, but every customer can give you something—straight talk. In doing so, she saves you time. If the sale is not to be and she lets you know it, the time you would have futilely spent on her can be spent elsewhere.

When you don't personalize relationships, you are just another salesman. There is no need for special consideration. If misrepresentation, deceit, and false encouragement are part of the customer's MO, you will be a target. Buyers are notorious for misleading salesmen. Until you've gotten out of the Non-Event, they see you as just another salesman with a handout. Why not mislead you? Your price is too high, your delivery is too slow, they don't like your customer service, and a hundred other complaints that have nothing to do with reality. They're just smoke screens.

I've known many salesmen who have worked years on a customer, and from day one they never had a chance. The bull's-eye wasn't visible because it was surrounded by a smokescreen. Smoke is deadly! It almost always gets you before the fire.

Personalize relationships and you still may not get the order, but you can throw away your gas mask. You can spend your time and effort on issues that are real.

CHAPTER 6

CREATE A NETWORK

The defect of equality is we desire it only with our superiors.

I cannot imagine existing in a world in which I was not surrounded by friends. When I started my business career as a sales representative I was given a lot of input as to the negatives that surrounded a sales job. It was said that if the customers didn't get to you, loneliness would.

Not if you are a Motivational Accelerator. Motivational Accelerators understand it's not any more difficult to build a friendship across the country than across the street. There is no law that states friends need to share the same paper boy.

As I reflected back on all the great salesmen I've known, a common thread ran through the fabric of their individual selling styles. No, it is not creativity, intelligence, sense of urgency, or communication skills. What they share with each other is an ability to build a successful network, a group of individuals who they motivate to support and sustain their efforts. They recognize they are not an island unto themselves. They realize no matter how great their individual talent, it pales in comparison to a supporting cast.

NO ONE DOES IT BETTER

Marty Edelston, CEO of the BOARDROOM Inc. and founder of Bottom Line Publications, has taken networking to new heights. He has built a publishing empire in large part by word of mouth. His targeted approach involves people talking to people, people meeting with people, people recommending people. Twice a month, he invites contributors to his publications to a gala dinner at the BOARDROOM. It appears that the purpose of the gathering is to share intellectual insights. In actuality, Marty Edelston uses the forum to expand his mailing list. Nothing wrong with that. The experience of a magnificent dinner with Marty Edelston makes every attendee desirous of returning. The strategy is simple, Marty treats you nicely and then asks for something from you—a name or two. When the request is made for you to offer up a few stimulating friends, you can't wait to oblige. Edelston understands that ten people know ten people who know ten people. The mailing list grows exponentially. Get enough names and before you know it, you have a readership of millions.

Motivational Accelerators understand that as they increase their involvement with others, their span of control broadens. Building a network can be one of the most important as well as personally satisfying things you do. It's critical because without a network, your success will be limited. It is emotionally satisfying because it involves expanding your relationships. An added bonus is it's easy to accomplish. If you want to meet new people, just ask. I've known very few individuals who weren't in search of a new pal.

Analyze any sales transaction and you will quickly identify that a number of individuals are involved. To draw an analogy, selling is akin to putting a puzzle together, and we should not attempt to do it unless we are sure we have all the pieces. Without each piece in place the puzzle is incomplete. From individuals at the account, to individuals in your organization, to others that hang on the periphery, anyone can make or break a sale. A Motivational Accelerator develops and motivates his supporting cast to perform at the highest possible level whenever his interests are at stake.

He understands that the bigger the team, the more diverse the talent, and the greater the probability of success. He also understands that when you have a supporting cast you can farm out all those little things to someone else. Let them take care of the minutiae while you focus on the big stuff that scores points.

The Motivational Accelerator also knows that a network does not exist by accident or neglect. It needs to be nourished and sustained. When someone does something for you, give something back. Methods of recognition can vary. Whether it's a letter of commendation, a book, a lollipop, a bottle of wine, a bag of cookies, or a hundred other things, your thoughtfulness will go a long way. It will tell a team member that his or her efforts have not gone unnoticed or unappreciated. In return, you will continue to receive favorable consideration. People will pick up the ball when you drop it. View everyone as a resource and your load will be lightened. Never underestimate the ability of anyone to perform on your behalf.

$300 RETURNS $30,000,000

Larry Leary is one of the best builders in Connecticut, and his commitment to quality, innovation, and giving his customers unsurpassed value made him a home buyer's dream come true. Who wouldn't want a Leary house? As it turned out, lots of people.

You see, even though Larry had been telling realtors and prospective clients he built great houses, nobody believed him. He had no track record. He had the reputation as the "home addition" guy, and even though his workmanship was everywhere, you couldn't find a Larry Leary house. I met Larry, and something about him made me believe he had the ability to build a great home. I contracted to have a house built.

Larry wouldn't have labeled himself a salesman, but he knew the principles. He understood the use of Accelerators and Positive Impactors. Whatever standard we agreed upon, he quickly ignored. He upgraded everything. He didn't care if he made a profit because he recognized this opportunity would make a statement about him.

My house would be a monument to Leary's ability to perform. The relationship became symbiotic right from the start. Larry needed my money and I needed his skill.

At the first opportunity, approximately a month into the project, Larry told me that instead of a wooden deck, he thought a raised flagstone patio would look better. The cost differential happened to be substantial but he would absorb it. His input accelerated me and I wanted to encourage him to continue to make those kinds of changes. A week later, I purchased two round-trip tickets to Puerto Vallarta with his name on them and gave him the use of my condominium there for a week.

A nice house quickly turned into an estate. Larry lived up to every expectation. He went from builder to friend and because of that I decided I would save the best for last. Upon completion of the house, I would make Larry the most sought after builder in the state. It wouldn't be difficult because I understood the value of testimonials; input given by someone else. For some reason, when another individual delivers the message, it becomes more credible, less biased, and of greater worth. I would testify for Larry Leary. Larry thought letting a member of his network spread the word was a good idea.

He completed the job and the house was terrific. I told Larry so, and he was happy to hear it but my praise did nothing for his bank account. Ten minutes of my time and $300 did. As a matter of fact, he went from "Larry who" to celebrity status overnight. Yes, I said overnight. Rather than keep my feelings to myself, I decided to share them with the community. Because I wanted to accelerate the process, the dinner party circuit wouldn't do, too slow and too fattening. I evaluated a number of possible Positive Impactors and made my choice. A week later, a half page ad appeared in the local paper. It read, "Thanks Larry Leary Construction Management for a terrific house and a wonderful building experience—The Sullivans." His phone started ringing that day and hasn't stopped.

Was his newfound popularity an accident? Not at all. I recently decided to buy a house in New Hampshire and retained a realtor to find me something suitable. Norma Fuller had just changed careers, had little real estate experience, and even fewer clients. I decided that if she performed, I would change all that. You know the drill. The newspaper ad read "Thanks Norma Fuller . . . !!! " Her phone started ringing that day.

Getting things accomplished doesn't always take hard work. Smart work is always better. It's all in understanding how the game is played. If you want a free pass to Disneyland you don't need to know Donald Duck. If you know cousin Leo, you're in.

Hardly a month goes by when I'm not contacted by an executive head hunter, looking to put me into a job somewhere in corporate America. The call never changes in the introductory phase. "I've been given your name by someone, who tells me you're the perfect candidate for this opportunity." They know nothing about me, but because another person said I was okay, I'm okay. Had I called them and suggested I was okay, they probably would have hung up.

I'll reiterate what I said about giving the network your utmost attention. That doesn't mean you need to take it to dinner every night, just show your supporters they are always in the forefront of your thoughts.

OH NO

As part of any speech I give on selling, I attempt to cement concepts with personal participation. For years, after talking about networking, I would offer myself up as recruit. I would tell the audience I would be happy to send a personalized autographed book to any customer of anyone present. They would have to pay the wholesale cost of the book plus shipping.

Even though I was sincere about the offer, I knew few would take me up on it. That was until I hit Seattle. After my speech a woman approached whom I had accompanied on her first sales call a decade earlier. I knew she would become a superstar and she had. Her reputation bordered on legend. When I made the offer I had no idea she was in the audience. "Action" was her middle name. We exchanged pleasantries as I broke out into a cold sweat. I am a man of my word and because of it, my future flashed in front of my eyes. I would be signing books until I reached social security. The vision was confirmed when she asked me if I could, for old times sake, wait around a few minutes. Sure, I said.

Twelve minutes later she returned with a xeroxed list of ninety-two customers' names and addresses. "I appreciate the offer," Julie said with a smile as she handed me a check. Now there is someone who understands the power of a network. I haven't made the offer since.

When you understand the power of a network you will build one posthaste. And when it is functioning like a well-oiled machine, life becomes beautiful.

CHAPTER 7

BECOME A BETTER COMMUNICATOR

Empty heads have long tongues

If I were asked to come up with a list of adjectives that accurately described a Motivational Accelerator, it would probably fill a page. If I were limited to just one synonym, it would be Communicator.

Everything a salesman does is for naught if it cannot be communicated to the buyer. The history books are filled with examples of people and organizations who failed for only one reason; they didn't understand how important it was to get the message out.

The lessons learned are a matter of record, so I'm amazed at how poorly many salesmen express themselves, verbally and in writing. It's apparent that they have no concept of the perception they create when their communication skills are lacking. There is a direct correlation between one's ability to express oneself and success. If you are unable to get knowledge from your brain past your lips, your climb up the ladder of success will approximate an assault on Everest.

Salesmen are paid to communicate! If you can't, your worth is marginal! Over the years, I've had the misfortune of listening to countless numbers of sales presentations that were ill-prepared, poorly given, and extremely boring. Within minutes after the salesman started, my thoughts took flight to a South

Pacific island. When the sales pitch was finished, and I was asked for the order, because I had not been mentally present, there was nothing I could say but "No!" The salesman obviously didn't comprehend that if my mind wasn't into it, my wallet wouldn't be either. As Ben Franklin said, "For the want of a nail the shoe was lost."

There are hundreds of activities that surround the process of getting something sold. If 99% of them are accomplished, and the salesman lets the communication link break, nothing happens. Everyone's effort is wasted.

Being able to articulate your thoughts clearly is critical. It's one of my hot buttons. Anyone who works for me will have to become an excellent communicator, and it is a prerequisite for long-term employment. I'm doing them a favor by forcing the issue.

I recognize that a lot of individuals shy away from public speaking. Research has discovered it is one of mankind's primary fears.

The Problem: If you are afraid of public speaking, you will avoid opportunities to do it, and in so doing, you will shortchange yourself and your company. The message needs to get out and the salesman must play the role of messenger.

The Opportunity: Once you recognize the need to become a better communicator, you will work on it. Practice makes perfect. As your abilities grow, your confidence will also. You'll become a walking presentation. It won't take long to realize it's as easy to address an audience of one hundred as it is one; and it's certainly more productive.

As you perform, you become a much more valuable asset. In addition, because so many salesmen are such poor communicators, you will stand out. Your customers will recognize your ability and see you as a resource they can use. You'll become part of their network.

FIREFIGHTER OR PUBLIC SPEAKER

Believe it or not, a majority of people would rather fight a blaze then give a speech. I've learned that from experience, on too many occasions. I remember one incident well. The protagonist arrived on my doorstep as a squeaky-clean, energetic salesman and informed me he wanted to conquer the world. I carved out a territory and decided the sooner I got him in action, the better.

I told him to set up a series of meetings, whereby he would introduce himself, give an information briefing on our company, and answer any questions that the audience had. At the time, I didn't realize he had never given a speech. I thought I had set a reasonable goal but in this case, his perception of the event approximated a climb up K-2 with anvils tied to his feet.

I decided to participate in the first one to show support and establish how a presentation should be conducted. As we set up the room for a group of eighty-five, I noticed he was sweating profusely. The temperature on the thermostat read sixty five, so I knew it had nothing to do with the room being overheated. The water dripping on the floor came from an anxiety attack. I recognized the symptoms and immediately asked if he had ever spoken in public. His cotton-mouthed response indicated he hadn't.

Alert! Alert! Alert!

I'm not sure how someone else would have handled the situation but I knew failure is no way to build confidence. As his mentor, it fell on me to extricate him. I told him I needed to talk to these guys about some changes in our product offering so I would take the first fifty minutes. When I was finished, I would introduce him. All he needed to do was give a brief background on himself and call it a day. The huge smile on his face told me my instincts had been correct.

Now, I prayed he wouldn't forget his name. He didn't, and as he gained confidence in the sound of his voice, he spoke beyond what I'd instructed. As we proceeded to give these presentations over a two-month period, the format never changed, with one exception. As he progressed, I would give him an ever-increasing portion of the program. One day, as we were setting up for our fifteenth encounter, he turned to me and confidently said, "I'll take this one on my own!"

A few years later I received a call from a friend who had witnessed his debut as a public speaker. She told me she'd just returned from a graphic arts conference, and although most of the speakers were terrible, one stood out. Could I guess who, she asked. I knew the answer.

This scenario is not atypical. In a profession that mandates an ability to speak, it is alarming how many salesmen can't. Instead of seeking opportunities to develop their skill they avoid them, and everyone is penalized because of it. Accept the fact that if you are going to achieve what you want in selling, being able to speak effectively is a prerequisite for success. Very few people are born articulate but with a few pointers and a lot of practice the transition will be quick.

Selling superstars understand that great communication involves more than the information that is passed from them to their audience. It also involves getting that information disseminated to the masses. For that to happen they know they need to communicate.

THE GRAPEVINE

Are you thinking about Napa Valley? Don't. The grapevine I'm talking about has nothing to do with vino. Our grapevine is a vehicle through which information is passed along, in many cases at supersonic speeds.

This is the Information Age! Billion dollar organizations have been created overnight by giving consumers products that allow them to communicate more quickly. Who wants to wait an hour to make contact when you can pull a phone out of your briefcase and do it instantaneously?

Recent events have shown that the quicker one can communicate, the more one will communicate. Look around you. We are bombarded by information. Everywhere! Twenty-four hours a day, seven days a week, 365 days a year, people are talking to us and about us. Much of it is "noise," and the delivery mechanisms, in many cases, are inane, but we are listening! Not only do we listen, but we pass along much of what we hear.

Motivational Accelerators understand how important a communication network is to their success. They want as many people to know about them as possible. They recognize that any individual effort in promoting themselves or their product can't compare to the collective effort of a support group. Get lots of people to say nice things about you. Let them express favorable opinions and accelerate the process. There is something about input coming from others that appears less self-serving. Tell people you're great and they'll think you're egotistical. Let someone else deliver the message, and it becomes a truth.

If you are going to be successful you need to get the word out. Use the grapevine. Get people talking about you. Let them deliver the superlatives. When you exhibit behaviors that are honest, credible, adventurous, thoughtful, kind, concerned, knowledgeable, and creative, people won't hesitate to paint a picture of you that generates interest in others.

They've heard you're unique. They'll want to meet you. The grapevine can facilitate the creation of a powerful image and much of the effort is supplied by others. Properly using the grapevine will open doors and deliver opportunities that you didn't know existed.

Once you understand the significance of the grapevine, you will take all precautions to protect your image within it. Proper fertilization (Accelerators) engender growth, while improper fertilization (Decelerators) kill.

Be advised that Decelerators move through the grapevine more quickly than Accelerators. It's unfair but true. In selling there are two types of buyers: The Apostle and the Terrorist. The Apostle is pleased with your performance and will spread the good word. The Terrorist, on the other hand, is displeased with what you've provided and will condemn you at every opportunity. The injustice lies with the fact that the Terrorist is ten times more likely to spread negatives than the Apostle is to spread positives.

Motivational Accelerators understand the principle and guard against any destructive input. If, for some reason, negative information about them is generated, they take immediate corrective action. Speed is of the essence. They flood the conduit of information with Accelerators to neutralize the Decelerator.

In the event it reaches the grapevine, it does so in a weakened state. The impact is lessened. Accelerators arrive shortly thereafter, and the damage will have been minimized. The Motivational Accelerator recognizes the potentially disastrous effects of negative publicity and does whatever is necessary to prevent it.

THE NON-ACCELERATOR

A Non-Accelerator's view of a grapevine is ten grapes. Abuse him, lie to him, ignore him, it doesn't matter: he won't talk. What happened yesterday will soon be forgotten and forgiven. No one else will know. Or will they? Wait a second, ten people know ten people who know ten people. That's considerably more than a bunch. An isolated incident soon becomes the talk of the town.

106

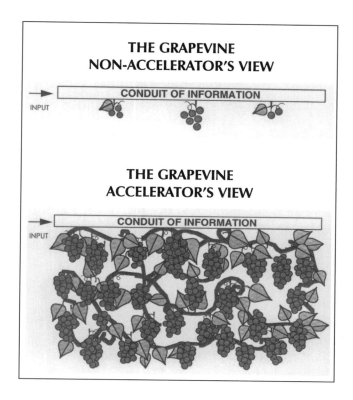

THE BIRTH OF A MEGAPHONE

I recently entered the post office and was greeted by the sound of a wailing patron. It was impossible to locate the source of the noise because she was surrounded by a half dozen listeners. I surmised she had just lost someone dear. As I drew closer, I discerned the noise was not so much a wail as it was an angry bark. The story was hardly front page news but her vicious condemnation of a local baker had everyone listening. (Terrorists have been known to exaggerate the facts to gain a sympathy vote.) As she told it, she had bought some bread that she discovered had leprosy. Her attempt to return it met with failure and as a consequence a Terrorist was born. A million dollar ad campaign would not have gotten the baker more publicity. Unfortunately, it was all bad.

ANTHONY PARINELLO

If you haven't been to the War Room in the Pentagon and wonder what that experience is all about, call Tony Parinello, the president of Parinello Inc. The activity level is about the same. He knows that to win any war, intelligence is a critical component for success. I have not met an individual in my military, business, or personal life who has a better understanding or operational capability to use the grapevine than Parinello.

Sit in his office for twenty minutes, and you will understand why AT&T has voted him customer of the year, ten years running. The phone never stops ringing, and Tony never stops calling. Information is received, analyzed, and dispatched to its proper place.

He is the executive equivalent of a switching device. Everything comes through him, and because of that, he sits atop a mountain of intelligence. Want to know something? Call Tony. Need to get your message out? Parinello is your man.

Success in selling involves awareness and because Tony Parinello has been fertilizing grapes forever, he is always a player.

CHAPTER 8

ESCAPE THE RUT OF MEDIOCRITY

Do not go where the path may lead; go instead where there is no path and leave a trail.

One of the rewards of having knowledge about something is periodically sharing it with others. Over the years, I have been involved in countless training sessions in the area of sales and marketing. Although each group differed in a variety of ways, I have observed there is one characteristic that remained constant—the ability to be creative. That's the good news. The bad news is that creativity, too often, is only seen in an academic setting.

Academia is a warm and loving place. Nobody gets fired there, at least not the students. They know that, so they go for broke. Unfortunately, much of what is created in the classroom never makes it to the streets.

For some reason, their open-minded approach to problem solving is an idiosyncratic characteristic relegated to intellectual settings. Once their educational experience is over, and they are back on the job, their creativity takes residence in the closet under lock and key. They crawl back into the same Non-Event rut they were in before, and go merrily, or not so merrily, on their way. Why? My guess is it has something to do with laziness or fear of failure. Laziness occurs because it's easier to do things the way they've always been done, no brain power needed. Just reach into that old bag of tricks and pull something out. No matter the customer has seen the trick a dozen times.

But what a Non-Accelerator doesn't understand, and a Motivational Accelerator does, is that the use of creativity in energizing relationships is not hard work, it's fun work. Exploring different ways to do things often results in uncovering new and better ways to do things. In the process of energizing your customer, you will energize yourself. Boredom will take flight.

You might say your unwillingness to be creative has nothing to do with being lazy, you just don't want to fail. I applaud your concern, but you should recognize that there is no chance of failing when being creative with a customer. The actual attempt at being creative may not win you an Academy Award, but the mere fact you tried to do something different will be an Accelerator on your scorecard. Successful selling involves your ability to make the statement, "I'm different." If you can't, you are running with the herd and that's a Non-Event.

Creativity will enable you to stand out. Look around you; the people and businesses that are succeeding are breaking the mold. Who says cappuccino doesn't sell in bookstores and rickshaws won't work in Coconut Grove? Are you wondering whether you can make your fortune in an art supplies shop? "Pepper Pete" Anderson will tell you, "not unless you also sell hot sauce." Bring a little ingenuity into your customer's world, and even if you don't solve the problem, you'll score big when it comes to setting yourself apart.

Need some help? Here are a few accelerating actions that I can guarantee will score you points.

ACCELERATING ACTIONS

- *Surprise pizza parties.*
- *Periodic delivery of something to eat, the more creative the better. You score with thoughtfulness and creativity.*

- *Make a list of important customers and their family members. Recognize anniversaries, births, birthdays, and special events.*
- *Free lesson of any kind: golf, tennis, skiing, etc.*
- *Send an autographed poster/picture of a favorite personality.*
- *Give a gift for their children. The size of the gift doesn't matter.*
- *Do something thoughtful for someone they hold dear.*
- *Use your network of friends to somehow get involved with your best customers.*
- *Invite a customer over for a cookout.*
- *Take a customer and spouse out to dinner.*
- *Get involved in sporting events such as softball or bowling leagues.*
- *Send a CD of a buyer's favorite artist.*
- *Send a postcard to customers while on vacation.*
- *Call a customer at home on the weekends just to see how he or she is doing.*
- *"Be My Guest" dinner certificate.*
- *Video rental gift certificates.*
- *Movie tickets.*
- *Award a trip to the mall with a gift certificate.*
- *Take a customer to his or her favorite sporting, arts, or entertainment event.*
- *Bring in ice cream, popsicles, or sodas on a hot day.*
- *Give a plant.*
- *Run sales contests.*
- *Give periodic gift baskets of chocolates, fruits, teas, coffee, gum, or candy.*
- *Lottery tickets.*
- *Picnic lunch at customer's office.*
- *Hot air balloon ride.*

- *Theme park tickets.*
- *Desserts for lunch time.*
- *Subscription to weekly sports newspaper or other periodicals of interest.*
- *Give home phone number to key customers for evening calls.*
- *Use theatrical themes for driving home the important aspects of a presentation.*
- *Involve "customer support personnel," such as office managers and administrative assistants, in promotions and entertainment.*
- *Give creative sales presentations.*
- *Bring a barbecue grill and have a cookout with your customer.*
- *Send a postcard if something reminds you of your customer.*
- *Use personal thank-you notes.*
- *Write letters commending your customer's employees.*
- *Use handwritten notes with articles, clippings, items of interest, etc.*
- *Order your customer personalized stationery.*
- *Ask customers who are publishing newsletters to allow you to contribute information.*
- *Follow-up interview after shipping their "first order" or any important piece of business.*
- *Regularly call your customer and thank her for the relationship.*
- *Arrange trips to your facility to educate your customer and show your hospitality.*
- *Get to know customers' employees. Work to remember names.*
- *When you are out of town, try to call from the airport to ask how everything is going.*
- *Apologize to customers in writing for blatant mistakes and follow up with a phone call.*
- *Handle all complaints immediately. Correct the situation as quickly as possible.*

- *Provide information on subjects pertinent to a customer's business.*
- *Help your customer with issues that transcend the business relationship.*
- *Do something nice for a customer's pet.*
- *Send a customer a small gift to enhance a vacation, such as suntan lotion.*

Creativity doesn't necessitate playing an accordion while giving the features, advantages, and benefits of your service in Swahili. It does mean coming up with stimulating alternatives to what is presently being done. If you are doing the same things as your competition, you lose.

Use your competitor as a benchmark for your actions. If they bring donuts, counter with corn dogs. I've found creative people take a simple act and make it an event by modifying it in some way. If you don't happen to be the creative type, use your network.

WHO WAS THAT MAN ON THE WATER BUFFALO?

Eric Weber, a highly successful businessman in upstate New York, became a legend by turning vacation photos into postcards and then sending them to his customers. The photos are so absurd and humorous that people can't wait for the next one to arrive. Needless to say, Eric is always in their thoughts. The card arrives, the corn pops, and Eric becomes a little wealthier.

As a Motivational Accelerator, you don't need to reinvent the wheel. Creative solutions are everywhere. Check out the Internet. Some of the most creative people in the world hang out there. Rip'em off. What matters is not where the creativity came from, but that it showed up. A good joke is told ten million times. What works in Burma may work in Mississippi. The world is becoming smaller and you have almost instant access to it. Another great place to get the creative juices flowing is at a flea market; there's tons of stuff and it's cheap.

I'LL TAKE THEM ALL

Michael Filgate, a creative thinker and head of North Shore Studios, understands the concept. One Sunday he called and invited my wife and I to a Sunday brunch. On the way to the quaint New England inn we passed a flea market. He asked if we minded stopping for a few minutes. As he pointed out, you just never know what you will find. Five minutes into the hunt he found his payday: toothbrushes for a quarter. One dentist's trash is a Motivational Accelerator's treasure. Michael Filgate bought the entire inventory. Do you have any idea how important clean teeth are to people, he asked. My immediate purchase of twenty-five rolls of discount dental floss indicated I did.

Are you thinking that it can't be this easy? A toothbrush for a relationship? A Motivational Accelerator understands that the product is not the Accelerator. The act is. It's one more thoughtful act among many that makes the difference. If the action is a little zany it will stand out and be remembered. Everytime it is, you score.

Recognize that the difference between success and failure can be very small. When all the big things are equal among competitors, a buyer has no choice but to look at the small stuff. The buyer's thought process is not complex. Two salesmen enter the arena. Both have all the bases covered. One is predictable and one is fun. Who gets the relationship? That's a rhetorical question.

HARTFORD. DRY RIBS? JOHN GRYMES!

I remember the sales call vividly. I was on a sales call with my area salesman with a very tough, unyielding buyer in Hartford. In the course of making small talk, the buyer commented that he had gone to school in Memphis. He continued by stating that the best ribs in the world come from the Rendezvous restaurant located in downtown Memphis. Anyone who has been to Memphis knows it has two celebrities: Elvis and dry ribs from the Rendezvous.

The buyer, after telling us we still would not get the business, started to discuss how much he missed those ribs. Thirty seconds later John excused himself from the table and went to a pay phone. He called the Rendezvous and placed an order for ribs to be air expressed to Hartford. The note inside said, "Thanks for taking time to hear our story. Your friends at IP." Yes, shortly thereafter, IP got the business. Without getting into any psychological analysis, here's what I think transpired.

The buyer, even though he said we wouldn't get the business, hadn't made up his mind. Buyers have been known to misrepresent the facts on occasion. In reality, he had been energized by John on previous calls and found himself close to Acceleration. Two Accelerators or one Impactor would do it.

Only a creative person would recognize that the death of a cow in Tennessee could lead to the birth of a relationship in Connecticut. John is a Motivational Accelerator but his choice of Impactor was not rocket science. The customer had identified something of importance and John acted on it, immediately. It's not surprising that when you give customers what they desire quickly and do it in a way that is different, very often they will give something in return, a relationship.

ONE ACT, ONE NEW HOUSE

For a few years I lived next to a highly successful advertising executive. He was a Motivational Accelerator par excellence. One snowy morning he called me to discuss a problem he was having at a major wine account. He thought he had made all the right moves but could not get a product manager to budge.

My philosophy has always been that when you hit an impasse, interject a little creativity. The Impactor came quickly. I invited him over and laid out the plan. We would adorn ourselves in summer attire, tank tops, sunglasses, and shorts, and have cocktails sitting at a picnic table in what turned out to be a major blizzard. On the table was a bottle of the company's product sitting in four inches of snow. The photo was shot and blown up to twenty-four by thirty-six inches. It was sent Federal Express to the intractable decision maker with a note. "Neither rain, nor snow, nor sleet, nor gloom of night will stay this adman from drinking your seltzer, Bob Lapple." Yes, he got the business.

I'll conclude my thoughts on creativity by being blunt. Get a new bag of tricks! Whatever the added cost, your customer will probably make up the difference by giving you a better lifestyle.

CHAPTER 9

STAND YOUR GROUND

To know what is right and not to do it is the worst cowardice.

When I reflect back on my twenty years of professional selling and attempt to identify what behavioral characteristics made the greatest impression on my customers, four come to mind:

- *Kindness*
- *Commitment*
- *Generosity*
- *Courage*

There is probably room for debate as to the level of emotional impact any of these actions engendered in a buyer, with one exception, Courage.

America is a society built around the concept that standing up for what you believe in separates the winners from the losers. It's the stuff of legend and great books. I don't know of anyone who read *A Milk Toast for All Seasons*.

In the world markets, backbone is traded as a precious commodity. It provides a foundation on which to build a relationship. Motivationally Accelerated selling requires a lot of courage. Superstars recognize that the more times they take action, the greater the opportunity for success, but also failure. They operate outside the comfort zone because they know that in selling, batting average means nothing! Making two hundred calls and closing on fifty is far better than making ten with five of them being a success. They do not let the fear of rejection inhibit their ability to act.

Motivational Accelerators recognize that rejection is not an indictment of their worth to the human race. It's merely a puddle on their journey to enlightenment and future success. How many times was Sir Lawrence Olivier rejected before he became an icon, and after he became one?

When you are rejected, read between the lines. I seriously doubt the message is "I hate you," it probably reads more like, "Not at this time." Have you decelerated lately? Is your customer waiting for three more Accelerators and a Positive Impactor? Evaluate your situation. Make whatever corrections are necessary and attack again. You'll find there are a plethora of buyers who reject for rejection's sake. They want to see what your counter will be. Have you ever heard about the path of least resistance?

I know of no one who wants a relationship with a coward! The proverbial "tail between your legs" doesn't elicit sympathy. It generates disgust. John Wayne stood his ground!

Motivational Accelerators operate under no misconception as to the traffic patterns in a relationship. There are no one-way streets. The nature of a successful partnership dictates that as you give, you shall receive. The concept is the cornerstone of any business. Your buyer expects to receive from her customers, and for her to think you should accept less is hypocrisy. Don't allow it to happen.

Your time and energy has value. The second a buyer accepts your service, she has established a contract with you. The fact that it is not a written contract makes no difference. What does matter is that you live up to your end of the agreement, so the buyer will live up to hers.

When you've done all the right things, you have earned a right to a portion of her business. If you are not getting it, it might be due to lethargy or ignorance on the buyer's part. She may be unaware of all that you have done. Educate her!

There is a cost associated with selling, and it must be covered. There is no risk in asking for the order. I cannot remember anyone trying to kill me for saying, "I want some of the business." In most cases, I received what I asked for, but when I didn't, I was no worse off than before I made the request. My ego may have been bruised but I recovered. When you compare the risk associated with selling with that of other professions, police work, fire fighting, or the military, it pales by comparison.

Why not let it all hang out? A turtle goes nowhere until it sticks its neck out. I suspect the same happens with a salesman.

BRUISED AND BEATEN

Menashe Cohen didn't become a legendary oriental rug dealer by playing jellyfish. As an Motivational Accelerator he has taken "customer-directed thought" to new heights. Spend twenty minutes with him and you'll be buying orientals for your golf cart. But as caring and considerate as he is, even this wonder boy has a breaking point.

The contact started innocently enough but shortly into the relationship; the sheep who called for service turned out to be rabid. When Menashe Cohen showed up at his palace to consummate a monumental sale, the individual's actions made Ivan the Terrible look like Bo Peep. His abusive demanor and caustic comments were reflective of someone who had gone loony. Menashe bit his lip in hopes of capitalizing on the mega-opportunity. He politely told the autocrat what he could do. The individual told him to shove it.

A month later Rasputin was back. The experience was repeated with the same results. On the third call, Cohen decided he had had enough and would stand his ground. He told the tyrant that his behavior was contemptible and whatever quote he had previously given was now tripled. A week later the individual called to apologize and told Menashe Cohen he liked and admired him and the new prices were fine.

There is only one absolute truth in selling: you are responsible for your actions. If you are willing to put forth the effort, success is guaranteed. With that success comes more than financial gain. As a Motivational Accelerator, you will receive the respect of the individuals you work with as well as the customer you sell.

Life will become very, very good!

CHAPTER 10

IN THE TRENCHES

Today is not the first day of the rest of your life. It's all there is of your life.

What you have just read is one man's view on selling. My knowledge of the subject did not come from a vision. It has evolved from experience over the past three decades, from buyers who have said yes, and those who have said no.

Through all of it, one undeniable truth comes out. Salesmen who have the greatest success recognize that the customer is not a side show. The customer brought the circus to town. They understand that to view it any other way engenders actions that shortchange the relationship. When the customer's time is no longer your time, and requests for help are acted upon slowly, when what he or she gives, to make you a success, is treated with callous indifference, you're in trouble.

Over the years I have seen salesmen who would have been ideal for the cover of the *Dale Carnegie Digest*, but they couldn't sell lemonade in the Mojave Desert. Physically they had it all, but somewhere in their sales orientation they developed an attitude that the customer was nothing more than a necessary nuisance. Because of that, their success was a fraction of what it could have been.

In contrast, I've seen superstars who have no formal selling education, appear disheveled, and present their cases with the sophistication of a jackhammer operator. Somehow they are still Masters of the Universe. Everyone wants to give them an order. Why? I've told you why. Believe it!

Certainly there is more to being successful than giving your customer a box of chocolates. Professionalism is part of the equation. Sales training is important for fine-tuning your selling techniques. If you haven't had any, get some, but recognize that knowing what to do and how to do it is worthless if a program of customer-directed activities doesn't follow. There are those that struggle with the concept that doing more gets you more. And there are those that don't.

ANSWERING A WAKE-UP CALL

Dear Steve:

Motivational Acceleration changed my life forever. I only became aware of this fact this past weekend and I decided to thank you for what you have done.

At thirty-five years old I was always a salesman even though, as you point out, it was never on my business card. I had been a singer in rock and roll bands, managed restaurants, bartended, waited on tables, and even became a hairdresser in order to meet women. Then, in 1995, for some reason I was offered a job with Cornerstone Marketing of America selling health insurance.

As it turned out, I knew absolutely nothing about selling. This became painfully obvious to me after my brief conversation with you. Let me refresh your memory.

I received a sales lead from our home office with your name on it and when I couldn't reach you by telephone, I sent you some information on our plan. I never heard from you. Finally, when I did reach you, I was infuriated by what you told me. "I would never do business with a company that was so unprofessional." One specific comment that angered me the most related to my send-ing our information in a plain #10 white envelope. I was mad. How could you not want to see me because of a stupid envelope? As I have done in the past, I reacted immediately and called you a few choice names. I took your comment very personally. What difference does an envelope make, I asked myself. Now I can only imagine whether you even looked at the information I sent. I now know that I would not have. Later that day I had still not insulted you enough so I sent you a letter with my inner-most feelings revealed in it.

What happened next came as a great surprise. You wrote me to apologize for insulting me when obviously it was I who had insulted you. Not only did I get an apology, but you sent me a copy of your book Selling at Mach 1. *I read it immediately and have read it many times, including on the plane home from Dallas this past week-end where I was honored for being one of the top twenty-five sales representatives nationwide. Out of 2,000 reps! I owe my life as it is now to my experience, as humiliating as it was, of being given a valuable lesson. When I don't have a clue as to what I'm talking about, just shut up and listen.*

Consider, at age thirty-five I had one year of college edu-cation and had never made more than $30,000 a year. In 1994 my tax return read $12,500. This past year my tax return read $108,000. This year I'm on track to dou-ble it. I never dreamed that having "Sales Representative" on my business card would actually mean my customers would view me as a real professional. Thanks to Motiva-tional Acceleration I am.

Sincerely,

Terry Johanesen

Note: The letter has merit only as a case study. A salesman struggling to succeed did not know how the game was played. Once he learned the rules, he had a choice to make. Do it or don't do it. He did and his life has changed. Whether it is forever is up to him.

Whatever the environment, future success for any individual will parallel his ability to adapt to change. The process starts with an evaluation. Whether it's daily, monthly, or yearly, you need to objectively measure where you are in your customer relationships. Call it a customer audit. Let the customer give you a report card on your performance. It can be as easy as calling him and asking where you can improve. Pay less attention to what he says than the enthusiasm with which he says it. If the news is good, it will establish a level of performance on which to build, and if it is bad, view it as a cathartic experience and adjust your behavior immediately.

Here is your action plan and it starts with the six questions: Who? What? When? Where? Why? and How?

Who: Start small! You may have a population of one hundred buyers you want to accelerate, but the first thing you need to do is build some confidence that Motivational Acceleration works. The process takes energy and commitment, all of which are given with the intent of getting a return on your investment.

Identify five of the most important people you want to sell to and start with them. In working with a smaller body of individuals you can better concentrate your efforts while reducing your resource exposure. As they respond to your efforts, your belief in the process will grow and you'll be ready for a quantum leap forward.

What: Start with a thank-you letter. There is always a reason to thank someone for something. When communication comes unexpectedly it will serve as an accelerator. Remember, I said start with five of your most important customers. You can thank them for the relationship, their time, consideration, or a myriad of other things. If you have been doing a great job for them, the thank-you will be just one more Accelerator that scores points.

If your efforts have been marginal up to that point, the thank you will have the effect of a cleansing agent. It will establish a reference point from which to Accelerate. Whatever you did prior to that can be forgotten if everything that follows is customer directed. Whatever else you decide to do after the thank you is up to you.

When: Intuition plays a large part in timing. My suggestion is that sooner is always better than later. At any given point, your customer may be on the verge of making a decision that will favor you or your competition. It's important that your actions be viewed with a certain naturalness, but if you aren't sure whether to do something now or in the future, do it now.

Where: Trying to decide "where" starts with evaluating your alternatives. Environment plays a large part in the significance of any action. As best you can, try to isolate your customers so that they receive the full impact of what you are doing. Getting them away from their place of business and all the irritants that go with it can make a major difference in how your message is received.

Contact your best customer, immediately, and invite him to a place that you know he likes so that he will be receptive to your invitation. Between his acceptance and the actual date, you will have plenty of time to come up with numerous Accelerators and Impactors that will make the statement: he is special and you are different.

Why: Experience is a wonderful teacher! As you experiment with different approaches, you will learn what works and what doesn't. Wasted effort will be minimized and every well-executed action will score.

How: Let me give you three things to consider before starting your Motivational Acceleration program.

1. **Speed:** In most things, there is a warm-up period, an introductory phase. You have to get through it before you can Accelerate. If you can't get out of the starting blocks, you'll never cross the finish line. Your customer was doing business

long before you arrived on the scene. Although you are full of enthusiasm and desire to "do the deal," much of what you will tell her has been heard before! Your consistent performance over time will determine the success of the relationship. Corn does not pop in two and a half minutes.

2. **Scope:** Every journey begins with an initial step. Identify what you feel most comfortable with and start there. As you achieve success and fine-tune your approach, you can take bigger strides.

3. **Focus:** Anyone who has been a salesman for any period of time recognizes that a majority of his success comes from a minority of his accounts. Your time, energy, and resources are finite. Identify where you appear to have the greatest opportunity for success and concentrate a major portion of your effort there. Treat everyone like you would want to be treated but treat some better than others. In reality, customers exist who are not worthy of your Motivationally Accelerated efforts and, therefore, should not receive them.

I think you have enough to get started, but let me make one final suggestion. Buy a full length mirror, and put it next to where you exit your residence. Each day, as you leave to take on the world, you might as well see how you are seen.

NOT BY ACCIDENT

What follows is not a unique case. It is happening everywhere. I relay it only because I watched it happen.

John Papa started his career as a salesman. Well, at least John knew he had sales capability. The title on his business card said mailboy. He delivered newspapers and mail, and he did it with such enthusiasm you thought you had received the *Declaration of Independence*. (He stood out.) It didn't take long for John to get noticed and promoted to the cashier's window. As usual, John took a mundane activity and turned it into an Event. Did I want to lunch with Malcolm

Forbes or experience the thrill of having John Papa cash my check? (He knew how to differentiate himself.)

Shortly after my first encounter with John, a position became available in the customer service group. It reported through me, and when I asked my operations manager if he had found a replacement, he stated he had a number of resumes and fifty phone calls about a guy named John Papa. (John was using his network.)

Even though he didn't carry the corporate academic qualifications, he got the job. Almost instantly he excelled. John knew who paid his salary—the customer. Every customer request received immediate attention. He developed a reputation for speed, and customers showed their appreciation with orders. He was promoted to supervisor, and within days he had instilled the same customer-directed enthusiasm to his subordinates. Promoted again!

I left the company, and hired him into an outside sales position. Soon after, another promotion to regional sales manager followed. His customers adore him, his competitors fear him, and I suspect before John hangs up his selling spurs, he'll write enough orders to fill a garbage dump. In my experience with John, I have yet to see a situation in which he played a part that didn't turn out to be an immediate success. It has nothing to do with how he looks or speaks.

What John possesses is the same attitude that makes any Motivational Accelerator successful. He understands that the customer relationship is not a means to an end, it is **The End.**

RECOMMENDED READING LIST

Bible
Bill of Rights
Boy Scout Creed
Declaration of Independence
Gettysburg Address
Torah
Constitution of the United States
Girl Scout Creed
Koran
Magna Carta
Ranger Handbook

ABOUT THE AUTHOR

Steve Sullivan started his professional career as a U.S. Army officer. His business career began as a sales representative. He is an internationally recognized authority on sales, leadership, and performance issues. He is the author of the two bestselling business books: *Selling at Mach 1* and Business Book of the Year *Leading at Mach 2*. His videos on Selling and Leadership are 1999 Vision Award winners. His thoughts on selling and leadership have been published in scores of periodicals worldwide. He holds a Bachelor of Arts degree in International Relations from the University of Florida and a Master's degree in Systems Management from the University of Southern California.